The Tempest

As Directed by
John Hirsch

Edited by
Elliott Hayes and
Michal Schonberg

CBC Enterprises
Toronto / Canada

Published by CBC Enterprises, a division of Canadian Broadcasting Corporation, Box 500, Station A, Toronto, Canada M5W 1E6, in association with Stratford Shakespearean Festival Foundation of Canada, Box 520, Stratford, Ontario, Canada N5A 6V2.

Publié par CBC Enterprises, une division de la Société Radio-Canada, C.P. 500, Succursale [A], Toronto (Ontario), Canada M5W 1E6, en collaboration avec la Stratford Shakespearean Festival Foundation of Canada, C.P. 520, Stratford (Ontario), Canada N5A 6V2.

CANADIAN CATALOGUING IN PUBLICATION DATA
Shakespeare, William, 1564-1616
   The tempest

ISBN 0-88794-115-X
1. Title
PR2833.A1 1983   822.3 3   C83-098564-5

General Manager/Directeur général:	Guy R. Mazzeo
Publisher/Éditeur:	Glenn Edward Witmer
Editor/Rédacteur en chef:	Betty Corson
Design/Design:	Leslie Smart and Associates Limited
Typesetting/Composition:	CompuScreen Typesetting Limited
Printer/Imprimeur:	D.W. Friesen and Sons Limited

Printed and bound in Canada

1 2 3 4 5 / 87 86 85 84 83

Distributed to the trade by:

Macmillan of Canada (a division of Gage Publishing Limited), Toronto

Contents

On Directing *The Tempest*. By John Hirsch   1

A Note to the Reader   9

The Cast   11

The Tempest   12

Stratford Festival Edition Emendations   104

Biographical Notes   117

On Directing *The Tempest*
By John Hirsch

I believe the highest creations of Shakespeare are, not his histories or tragedies, but his romances. These are really fairy tales, in the sense that child psychologist Bruno Bettelheim uses the term: simple and enchanting representations of profound human experiences that touch the very roots of social, religious, and individual problems.

The romance draws from both comedy and tragedy. It is a hybrid form of drama that expands the limitations of probability and allows a freedom within the play to explore the theatricality inherent in it. It is within the romance that different forces are brought together, good and evil, age and youth, innocence and knowledge, all the elements of air, earth, water, and fire; beauty and baseness; love and hatred; jealousy and generosity.

The romance points to the interconnection between the comic and the tragic. It is not a clearly defined genre like the comedy or the tragedy, both of which are anchored in reality and where the purpose and expectation are anticipated and the method and outcome are clear.

Romance is much closer to comedy, of course, because of the festive and comic elements that are present; but it differs, particularly in *The Tempest,* because of the impending darker forces and the proximity of tragedy, which does not occur only because of the influence of both natural and supernatural forces. In the romance the real and often harsh possibilities of life are seen in a purer light than in comedy, which allows for more relevant contemplation of their consequences and creates a greater resonance for each action.

The romance is comparable to someone who is both a realist and an artist: someone who has not led a sheltered life, who is aware of the strictures of reality and the need for compromise, and yet at the same time as an artist is always seeking an escape into an environment where he can let his imagination roam without restrictions. He is looking for an ideal (especially in a theatre as large and complex as the Stratford Festival, where one would like to make things happen by waving a magic wand).

I have spent thirty years in the theatre, longer if I were to include the passive experience of my childhood, such as attending plays, reading them, and simply observing life as it unfolds around me. You might say that I have spent my lifetime preparing to meet the challenge or, rather, accept the challenge of the romance plays of Shakespeare. It is the same way an actor

prepares all his life in order to play the role of Prospero or Othello or Lear.
I directed a major production of *The Tempest* at the Mark Taper Forum in Los
Angeles a couple of years ago and some may be surprised that I would want
to do it again, but this is an expression of the fact that as an artist I have not
finished.

No production of such a play can be definitive; no production can exhaust
the possibilities of this play. There is a constant process of discovery as a
director works with different actors, different designers, as the play adapts to
different spaces. There is a constant examination and re-examination of the
text as the artist finds out more about himself and the artist he is dealing
with, even though their life experiences are three and a half centuries apart.

It is relevant here to discuss the preparation I go through as a director
when approaching *The Tempest*. The first consideration is the text itself, and a
study of the period in which it was written. It is necessary to come to an
understanding of Shakespeare's concerns, his world view, the influences upon
his life, his frame of reference, and his possible sources. I search for other
sources, which I share with those who are working with me, sources that will
illuminate *The Tempest*: Ovid's *Metamorphoses*, Virgil's *Aeneid*. We read Bruno
Bettelheim's *Sources of Enchantment*, and we view Bergman's wonderful film *The
Magic Flute*.

This is a nurturing process, during which I feed myself germinal ideas by
drawing upon sources from any and all areas of human endeavour, both
artistic and non-artistic. And later on, in order to make certain points clearer,
I use this source material to illustrate and emphasize the ideas I am trying to
put across. I spend an extended period reading the text and these other
sources over and over again, searching for the meaning of the words,
examining the structure of the speeches, finding the various levels of meaning
through a deep analysis of the text.

We are dealing with a poet. There is no padding in the writing; it's all
concentrated and every word counts. Every "yea," "o," and "no" must be
investigated. An "o" may precisely mark the place where emotion is
expressed. Every "no" is not the same – one might be a "no" of denial, another
a "no" meaning "on the contrary." One of the secrets to performing
Shakespeare is that the actors must commit themselves to the playwright.
Their performances will become easier as they learn to trust the words, and
express them simply while understanding completely each phrase, pause, and
inflection. Shakespeare need not be so difficult. If the actors simply speak,
describe, and explain, the emotional life and intentions will take care of
themselves.

I also search for parallels within Shakespeare's other plays. For example, I
read Bottom's speech in *Midsummer Night's Dream* when he wakes up from his
dream, and compare it to the Boatswain's speech in *The Tempest* when he comes
at the end of the play and tells everyone that he had thought the ship had
split apart, but woke to find it even better than it was before.

This is a pleasurable and productive phase, and when this basic and essential work has been done, I look for and wait for the resonances within my own mind. I become totally preoccupied with the text. I eat, sleep, and drink thinking of it.

Simultaneously, I begin to think of how the magic will be created in physical, spatial, visual, and aural terms. In *The Tempest* the magic is created from the very outset as the audience files into a theatre filled with the ominous sounds of an angry ocean. The storm is created by the huge, dark, billowing sail that immediately transports the audience into the middle of a raging tempest, which culminates with the mad rush of the seafarers abandoning ship when the theatre is suddenly plunged into darkness.

Next, the lights come up on an empty stage representing the peaceful surroundings of Prospero's magic island. The lighting has changed from a mysterious blue to the warm ambers of sunlight. From this point on, the stage remains practically bare except for the books of magic which are Prospero's most precious property.

The spare and simple costumes of Prospero and Miranda contrast with the elaborate clothes of the court party. However, during the scenes when Prospero performs his magic in the feast and the Masque, the courtiers pale in comparison to the wonder conjured up by his magic. This is also reflected in the costumes of the fantastic fauna that spring from Prospero's imagination.

Throughout the play, music has an essential role in contributing to the heightened atmosphere that exists on the island, as does the choreography.

No single element, however important, should be allowed to compete with the power of the words. The poetry of the piece is always at the heart of the production.

The Tempest is unquestionably one of Shakespeare's most important expressions concerning existence, responsibility, and human tragedy. It distills human experience and presents it in a simple and mythical fashion.

It is the journey through the wilderness that begins in the Bible:

> And there came a voice from Heaven saying "Thou art my beloved Son, in whom I am well pleased." And immediately the spirit driveth him into the wilderness.
>
> And he was there in the wilderness forty days, tempted of Satan; and was with the wild beasts; and the angels ministered unto him.

And like all good fairy tales, *The Tempest* presents a spiritual journey. We sometimes think fairy tales are very simple, but of course they are not. They always deal with matters of utmost importance – life and death, loss and change, rites of passage, growing up. Young children understand such sophisticated matters when presented with them on a subconscious level.

While travelling abroad several years ago, I found myself sitting on a bus with a mother and her young child. As we passed under a bridge, the child jumped up in his seat and cried, "Train!" I felt certain that the child was seeing a train for the very first time in his life. His joy made all of us passengers see that train as if we had never seen one before. Shakespeare has a similar effect on us. He peels the layers from our eyes so that we see the world around us anew. He fills us with the same wonder that he experienced about the joys and tragedies of being mortal.

When I think of that childlike sense of wonder, I am reminded of the words of Goethe's mother, a master storyteller herself, talking of her son's wonder:

> "Air, fire, water and earth I presented to him as beautiful
> princesses, and everything in all nature took on a deeper
> meaning," she reminisced. "We invented roads between stars,
> and what great minds we would encounter. He devoured me
> with his eyes; and if the fate of one of his favourites did not go
> as he wished, this I could see from the anger in his face, or his
> efforts not to break out in tears. Occasionally he interfered by
> saying "Mother, the princess will *not* marry the miserable tailor,
> even if he slays the giant," at which I stopped and postponed the
> catastrophe until the next evening. So my imagination was often
> replaced by his; and when the following morning I arranged fate
> according to his suggestions, he said, "You guessed it, that's how
> it came out," he was all excited, and you could hear his heart
> beating.

In *The Tempest,* Miranda is full of that same wonder. She is like the little boy on the bus.

Why does Miranda's attention wander while her father tells her the entire family history? She is not bored, as she is sometimes played. The text just does not support this. Rather, she is mesmerized by the sea and the tempest her father has conjured up.

> And now I pray you, sir, –
> For still 'tis beating in my mind, –
>   your reason
> For raising this sea-storm.

The only human she knows is her father, so she might reasonably assume that all men look like him. Imagine her surprise when she first sees Ferdinand. Entirely unlike her father in appearance, he really *is* an inhuman spirit to her. Like the boy on the bus, it is impossible for Ferdinand and Miranda to be too innocent or too filled with wonder towards each other and the fantastic world around them. In the entire play, only their relationship exists outside the realm of power politics, of the exploiter and the exploited. Paragons of virtue, their love is absolutely pure. Since their bond to one another exists by choice, their mutual consent gladly to serve each other sharply contrasts with the master-slave relationships that are in operation among the other characters in the play. Theirs is a model of an ideal human relationship.

Some critics contend that the sole function of *The Tempest*'s clowns is to provide comic relief. Stephano, Trinculo, and Caliban are certainly funny, but they do much more than entertain the audience. Their machinations precisely mirror Sebastian and Antonio's conspiracy as well as Prospero's expulsion from Milan. *The Tempest*'s comic triumvirate is essential to the evolution of the play's political theme.

Although evident throughout the play, the corrupting nature of power is perhaps clearest in Stephano. Since we know that he had no power prior to the shipwreck, it is quite simple to trace the way that power transmutes his character. Being half-monster, Caliban is the basest of all the creatures in the play.

Stephano and Trinculo wander through the island.
Caliban offers them food.

I prithee let me bring thee where crabs grow;
And I with my long nails will dig thee pig-nuts.
Show thee a jay's nest, and instruct thee how
To snare the nimble marmoset. I'll bring thee
To clustering filberts, and sometimes I'll get thee
Young scamels from the rock. Wilt thou go with me?

He then tempts them with power.

Prithee, my King, be quiet. See'st thou here,
This is the mouth o' the cell. No noise, and enter.
Do that good mischief, which may make this island
Thine own for ever, and I, thy Caliban,
For aye thy foot-licker.

Trinculo and Stephano quickly sink to his level (literally doing so in their trek through the cesspool). They become as filthy as he and, as they get drunk, just as greedy and violent. Their increasing lust for blood, riches, and absolute power is less humorous than it is frightening. They become willing to murder and even threaten each other's lives.

The city, Milan, is corrupt by its very nature. Power corrupts and Prospero had become nauseated by it—hence his decision to abandon his ducal responsibilities for the study of "liberal arts." His salvation depends on it. The result is his fall and expulsion, though he forgets that he brought it upon himself and is partially responsible.

The Tempest makes a profound statement about human responsibility: what the individual owes society and how this duty cannot be evaded. However imperfect society may be, one cannot live outside it, but must return to it. Prospero's situation is similar to Jonah's. Refusing God's order to preach against Nineveh, Jonah tried to run away, but God threw him into the sea where he was swallowed by the whale. Finally saved, Jonah then decided to follow God's will. Prospero's predicament is precisely the same. His preference of his studies to the affairs of state led to his banishment. He finally realizes, however, that he cannot run away, but must return.

In his commonwealth speech, Gonzalo wonders about the possibility of a perfect state.

> Had I plantation of this isle, my lord, – . . .
> And were the King on't, what would I do? . . .
> I' th' commonwealth I would by contraries
> Execute all things. For no kind of traffic
> Would I admit, no name of magistrate.
> Letters should not be known. Riches, poverty,
> And use of services, none. Contract, succession,
> Bourn, bound of land, tilth, vineyard, none.
> No use of metal, corn, or wine, or oil.
> No occupation; all men idle, all,
> And women too, but innocent and pure.
> No sovereignty – . . .
> All things in common nature should produce
> Without sweat or endeavour. Treason, felony,
> Sword, pike, knife, gun, or need of any engine
> Would I not have; but nature should bring forth
> Of its own kind all foison, all abundance,
> To feed my innocent people. . . .
> I would with such perfection govern, sir,
> To excel the Golden Age.

It is the golden age of Ovid in *The Metamorphoses*.

> The first millennium was the age of gold:
> The living creatures trusted one another;
> People did well without the thought of ill:
> Nothing forbidden in the book of laws,
> No fears, no prohibitions read in bronze,
> Or in the sculptured face of judge or master.
> Even the pine tree stood on its own hills,
> Nor did it fall to sail uncharted seas:
> All that man knew of earth were shores of homes,
> No cities climbed behind high walls and bridges:
> No brass-lipped trumpets called, nor clanging swords,
> Nor helmets marched the streets, country and town
> Had never heard of war: and seasons travelled
> Through the years of peace. The innocent earth

Learned neither spade nor plow; she gave her
Riches as fruit hangs from the tree: grapes
Dropping from the vine, cherry, strawberry
Ripened in silver shadows of the mountain;
Springtime the single season of the year.

As we dream of a perfect society, *The Tempest* asks the question, "How does one live in present society?" It is one of those questions without an answer. Equally, however, the search for perfection, the striving itself (even though the attainment of perfection is impossible), is one of those traits that defines what it is to be a human being. Hope springs eternal; we hope against hope.

The Tempest does not end nearly as happily as some of Shakespeare's pastoral plays, such as *As You Like It*. Prospero has given up Miranda, abjured his studies, and decided to return to Milan, "where every third thought shall be my grave." On his island he has transformed some of the personal relationships by forgiving his antagonists. Reconciliation follows, and the play ends with the characters brought together in a spirit of sacred communion.

Yet, all is not well. Milan lurks over the horizon. Affairs there are no doubt the same as they were twelve years earlier. Power politics and corruption continue to reign unabated. Shakespeare will not allow us to believe that Prospero's return to "civilization" will be easy or happy.

In tragedy the old order is restored; in comedy a new order is created. In *The Tempest* the requirements of the comedy are met through the marriage of Ferdinand and Miranda and the old order is restored when Prospero recovers his dukedom, and with it the responsibilities of a ruler. And yet all the characters return to the real world of Milan. There is no escape from reality.

The final communion on stage extends throughout the theatre, which is precisely what always should occur between actor and audience. The characters have learned to better understand themselves, but so has the audience. Since *The Tempest* is filled with theatrical metaphors, it is especially appropriate that it end with the open admission of its theatrical artifice. So, it is not Prospero who speaks the Epilogue, but the actor who plays him.

The theme of freedom is everywhere in the play. Caliban yearns for it; Ariel remembers when he had it and longs for its return. There is also the sense of freedom that arises from finding oneself and casting off false conceptions of self. Freedom is also present in two more subtle forms. Only thought is free and death brings final liberation from worldly problems and conundrums. Prospero frees both Caliban and Ariel, and when he says "every third thought shall be my grave," he also anticipates his own ultimate freedom.

John S. Hinnah

A Note to
the Reader

The text used in the Stratford Festival Edition of *The Tempest* is based upon the Globe Text, with reference to the First Folio. It incorporates generally accepted modern spellings and punctuations.

A glossary of Elizabethan and unfamiliar terms appears at the bottom of the pages.

The Act and Scene numbers are given at the top of each right-hand page. The Scene numbers enclosed in brackets in the right-hand margin indicate the way in which the play was divided for rehearsal purposes at Stratford. During a performance the stage manager would use these Scene numbers to call light, orchestra, and sound cues.

Also in the right-hand margin is the over-all numerical delineation; the Stratford Festival Edition delineation is enclosed in brackets. The SFE line numbers refer the reader to a set of emendations at the end of the text. These emendations include word changes, line changes, cuts, and additions that were made specifically for the 1982 Stratford Festival Production of *The Tempest*.

Sharry Flett as Miranda and Miles Potter as Caliban

The 1982 Stratford Festival Production of

The Tempest

Directed by John Hirsch
Designed by Desmond Heeley
Music by Stanley Silverman
Lighting Designed by Michael J. Whitfield

The Cast (In Order of Appearance)

Ship's Master	Deryck Hazel
Boatswain	Shaun Austin-Olsen
Alonso, King of Naples	Richard Curnock
Sebastian, his brother	Richard Monette
Antonio, the usurping Duke of Milan, brother of Prospero	Colin Fox
Adrian, a lord	Peter Waisberg
Gonzalo, an honest old counsellor	Lewis Gordon
Prospero, the rightful Duke of Milan	Len Cariou
Miranda, Prospero's daughter	Sharry Flett
Ariel, an airy spirit	Ian Deakin
Caliban, a savage, deformed slave	Miles Potter
Ferdinand, Alonso's son	Jim Mezon
Trinculo, a jester	John Jarvis
Stephano, a drunken butler	Nicholas Pennell
Iris	Irene Neufeld
Ceres	Loreena McKennitt
Juno	Anita Noel-Antscherl

Mariners,	Richard Binsley	Deryck Hazel	Anita Noel-Antscherl
Shades,	Nicolas Colicos	Shane Kelly	Paul Punyi
Monsters	Curzon Dobell	Beverly Kreller	Astrid Roch
and	Peter Donaldson	Anne McKay	Michael Simpson
Attendants	Maurice E. Evans	Loreena McKennitt	Craig Walker
	Christopher Gibson	Irene Neufeld	Peter Zednik

Assistant Director:	William Peters
Special Movement by:	John Broome
Stage Manager:	Michael Shamata
Assistant Stage Managers:	Michael Benoit, Victoria Klein, Jill Orenstein
Assistant Designer:	Polly Scranton Bohdanetsky

Scene 1

*On a ship at sea: a tempestuous noise of thunder
and lightning heard.*

Enter a Ship-Master, and a Boatswain

Master   Boatswain!   [1-67]
Boatswain Here Master. What cheer?
Master   Good. Speak to the mariners! Fall to't, yarely, or
            we run ourselves aground, bestir, bestir!   *Exit*

Enter Mariners

Boatswain Heigh, my hearts, cheerly, cheerly, my hearts! Yare,
            yare! Take in the topsail. Tend to the Master's
            whistle. Blow till thou burst thy wind, if room
            enough!

Enter Alonso, Sebastian, Antonio, Ferdinand, Gonzalo, and others

Alonso   Good boatswain, have care! Where's the Master?
            Play the men.   10
Boatswain I pray now keep below.
Antonio   Where is the Master, Boatswain?
Boatswain Do you not hear him? You mar our labour, keep
            your cabins! You do assist the storm.

[Scene 1] : All numbers in brackets refer to Emendations,   1.   **Boatswain:** pronounced Bos'n
         pp. 104-14. See also Note, p. 9.   3.   **yarely:** swiftly

Gonzalo	Nay, good, be patient.
Boatswain	When the sea is. Hence! What cares these roarers for the name of king? To cabin, silence! Trouble us not.
Gonzalo	Good, yet remember whom thou hast aboard.
Boatswain	None that I more love than myself. You are a counsellor, if you can command these elements to silence, and work the peace of the present, we will not hand a rope more, use your authority! If you cannot, give thanks you have liv'd so long, and make yourself ready in your cabin for the mischance of the hour, if it so hap. Cheerly, good hearts! Out of our way, I say. *Exit*
Gonzalo	I have great comfort from this fellow. Methinks he hath no drowning mark upon him, his complexion is perfect gallows. Stand fast, good Fate, to his hanging, make the rope of his destiny our cable, for our own doth little advantage. If he be not born to be hang'd, our case is miserable. *Exeunt*

20

30

Re-enter Boatswain

Boatswain	Down with the topmast! Yare, lower, lower, bring her to! Try with main-course. (*A cry within.*) A plague upon this howling! They are louder than the weather, or our office.

Re-enter Sebastian, Antonio, and Gonzalo

	Yet again? What do you here? Shall we give o'er and drown, have you a mind to sink?
Sebastian	A pox o' your throat, you bawling, blasphemous, incharitable dog!
Boatswain	Work you then.
Antonio	Hang, cur, hang, you whoreson, insolent noise-maker! We are less afraid to be drown'd than thou art.
Gonzalo	I'll warrant him for drowning, though the ship were no stronger than a nutshell, and as leaky as an unstanched wench.
Boatswain	Lay her a-hold, a-hold set her two courses off to sea

40

---

23. **hand:** handle
29. **complexion:** face
32. **advantage:** help

again, lay her off.

Enter Mariners wet

Mariner	All lost! To prayers, to prayers, all lost!	50
Gonzalo	The King, and Prince, at prayers! Let's assist them,	
	For our case is as theirs.	
Sebastian	I'm out of patience.	
Antonio	We are merely cheated of our lives by drunkards.	
	This wide-chopp'd rascal,–would though might'st lie drowning	
	The washing of ten tides!	
Gonzalo	He'll be hanged yet,	
	Though every drop of water swear against it,	
	And gape at wid'st to glut him.	
	(*A confused noise within:* 'Mercy on us!' –	
	'We split, we split!' – 'Farewell my wife and children!'–	60
	'Farewell, brother!' – 'We split, we split, we split!')	
Antonio	Let's all sink with the King.	
Sebastian	Let's take leave of him. *Exeunt Antonio and Sebastian*	
Gonzalo	Now would I give a thousand furlongs of sea for	
	an acre of barren ground, long heath, brown firs,	
	any thing! The wills above be done, but I would	
	fain die a dry death. *Exeunt*	

---

55. **wide-chopp'd:** wide-mouthed

56. **ten tides:** pirates were hanged on the shore and left there until three tides washed over them.

Colin Fox as Antonio and Richard Monette as Sebastian

Scene 2

The island. Before Prospero's cell.

Enter Prospero and Miranda

Miranda   If by your art, my dearest father, you have
Put the wild waters in this roar, allay them.
The sky, it seems, would pour down stinking pitch,
But that the sea, mounting to th' welkin's cheek,
Dashes the fire out. O, I have suffer'd
With those that I saw suffer! A brave vessel,
Who had, no doubt, some noble creature in her,
Dash'd all to pieces! O, the cry did knock
Against my very heart! Poor souls, they perish'd.
Had I been any god of power, I would   10
Have sunk the sea within the earth, or ere
It should the good ship so have swallow'd, and
The fraughting souls within her.

Prospero   Be collected,
No more amazement. Tell your piteous heart
There's no harm done.

Miranda   O, woe the day!

Prospero   No harm.
I have done nothing but in care of thee,
Of thee, my dear one, thee, my daughter who
Art ignorant of what thou art, nought knowing
Of whence I am, nor that I am more better
Than Prospero, master of a full poor cell,   20
And thy no greater father.

Miranda   More to know
Did never meddle with my thoughts.

Prospero   'Tis time
I should inform thee farther. Lend thy hand,
And pluck my magic garment from me. – So,

Lays down his mantle

Lie there, my art. Wipe thou thine eyes. Have comfort.

---

4.   **welkin:** sky

THE TEMPEST
STRATFORD ONTARIO

MIRANDA

WHEELER / 82

	The direful spectacle of the wreck, which touch'd

The direful spectacle of the wreck, which touch'd
The very virtue of compassion in thee,
I have with such provision in mine art
So safely ordered, that there is no soul,
No, not so much perdition as an hair.   30
Betid to any creature in the vessel
Which thou heard'st cry, which thou saw'st sink.
  Sit down,
For thou must now know farther.
Miranda   You have often
Begun to tell me what I am, but stopp'd
And left me to a bootless inquisition,
Concluding 'Stay: not yet.'
Prospero   The hour's now come.
The very minute bids thee ope thine ear.
Obey, and be attentive. Canst thou remember
A time before we came unto this cell?
I do not think thou canst, for then thou wast not   40
Out three years old.
Miranda   Certainly, sir, I can.
Prospero By what? By any other house or person?
Of any thing the image tell me, that
Hath kept with thy remembrance.
Miranda   'Tis far off,
And rather like a dream than an assurance
That my remembrance warrants. Had I not
Four or five women once that tended me?
Prospero Thou hadst, and more, Miranda. But how is it
That this lives in thy mind? What seest thou else
In the dark backward and abysm of time?   50
If thou remember'st aught ere thou cam'st here,
How thou cam'st here thou mayst.
Miranda   But that I do not.
Prospero Twelve year since, Miranda, twelve year since,
Thy father was the Duke of Milan and
A prince of power.
Miranda   Sir, are not you my father?
Prospero Thy mother was a piece of virtue, and
She said thou wast my daughter; and thy father
Was Duke of Milan, and his only heir
A princess, no worse issued.

---

26. **direful:** dreadful
35. **bootless:** unprofitable

Miranda	O the heavens!
	What foul play had we, that we came from thence? 60
	Or blessed was't we did?
Prospero	Both, both, my girl.
	By foul play, as thou say'st, were we heav'd thence,
	But blessedly holp thither.
Miranda	O, my heart bleeds
	To think o' the teen that I have turn'd you to, [64]
	Which is from my remembrance! Please you, farther.
Prospero	My brother and thy uncle, call'd Antonio –
	I pray thee, mark me, that a brother should
	Be so perfidious! He, whom next thyself
	Of all the world I lov'd, and to him put
	The manage of my state, as at that time 70
	Through all the signories it was the first,
	And Prospero the prime Duke, being so reputed
	In dignity, and for the liberal arts
	Without a parallel; those being all my study,
	The government I cast upon my brother,
	And to my state grew stranger, being transported
	And rapt in secret studies. Thy false uncle –
	Dost thou attend me?
Miranda	Sir, most heedfully.
Prospero	Being once perfected how to grant suits,
	How to deny them, who t'advance, and who 80
	To trash for over-topping; new created
	The creatures that were mine, I say, or changed 'em,
	Or else new form'd 'em; having both the key,
	Of officer and office, set all hearts i' th' state
	To what tune pleas'd his ear, that now he was
	The ivy which had hid my princely trunk,
	And suck'd my verdure out on't. Thou attend'st not!
Miranda	O, good sir, I do.
Prospero	I pray thee, mark me.
	I thus neglecting wordly ends, all dedicated
	To closeness and the bettering of my mind 90
	With that which, but by being so retir'd,
	O'er-priz'd all popular rate, in my false brother
	Awak'd an evil nature, and my trust,
	Like a good parent, did beget of him
	A falsehood, in its contrary as great

68. **perfidious:** treacherous
71. **signories:** territories
87. **verdure:** greenness, freshness

As my trust was, which had indeed no limit,
A confidence sans bound. He being thus lorded,
Not only with what my revenue yielded,
But what my power might else exact, like one
Who having into truth, by telling of it,   100
Made such a sinner of his memory
To credit his own lie, he did believe
He was indeed the Duke, out o' th' substitution
And executing th' outward face of royalty
With all prerogative. Hence his ambition growing –
Dost thou hear?

Miranda   Your tale, sir, would cure deafness.

Prospero To have no screen between this part he play'd
And him he play'd it for, he needs will be
Absolute Milan. Me, poor man, my library
Was dukedom large enough. Of temporal royalties   110
He thinks me now incapable; confederates –
So dry he was for sway wi' the King of Naples
To give him annual tribute, do him homage,
Subject his coronet to his crown, and bend
The dukedom yet unbow'd, – alas, poor Milan!
To most ignoble stooping.

Miranda   O the heavens!

Prospero Mark his condition, and th' event, then tell me
If this might be a brother.

Miranda   I should sin
To think but nobly of my grandmother,
Good wombs have borne bad sons.

Prospero   Now the condition.   120
This King of Naples, being an enemy
To me inveterate, hearkens my brother's suit,
Which was, that he, in lieu o' th' premises
Of homage, and I know not how much tribute,
Should presently extirpate me and mine
Out of the dukedom, and confer fair Milan,
With all the honours, on my brother. Whereon,
A treacherous army levied, one midnight
Fated to th' purpose, did Antonio open
The gates of Milan, and, i' th' dead of darkness,   130

---

122. **inveterate:** established by continuance   **Miranda and Len Cariou**

125. **extirpate:** to root out   **as Prospero ▶**

	The ministers for th' purpose hurried thence	
	Me, and thy crying self.	
Miranda	Alack, for pity!	
	I, not remembering how I cried out then,	
	Will cry it o'er again. It is a hint	
	That wrings mine eyes to 't.	
Prospero	Hear a little further,	
	And then I'll bring thee to the present business	
	Which now's upon's; without the which, this story	
	Were most impertinent.	
Miranda	Wherefore did they not	
	That hour destroy us?	
Prospero	Well demanded, wench.	
	My tale provokes that question. Dear, they durst not,	140
	So dear the love my people bore me; nor set	
	A mark so bloody on the business; but	
	With colours fairer painted their foul ends,	
	In few, they hurried us aboard a bark,	
	Bore us some leagues to sea, where they prepar'd	
	A rotten carcass of a butt, not rigg'd,	
	Nor tackle, sail, nor mast. The very rats	
	Instinctively have quit it. There they hoist us,	
	To cry to th' sea, that roar'd to us; to sigh	
	To th' winds, whose pity, sighing back again,	150
	Did us but loving wrong.	
Miranda	Alack, what trouble	
	Was I then to you!	
Prospero	O, a cherubin	
	Thou wast that did preserve me. Thou didst smile,	
	Infused with a fortitude from heaven,	
	When I have deck'd the sea with drops full salt,	
	Under my burthen groan'd, which rais'd in me	
	An undergoing stomach, to bear up	
	Against what should ensue.	
Miranda	How came we ashore?	
Prospero	By Providence divine,	
	Some food we had, and some fresh water, that	160
	A noble Neapolitan, Gonzalo,	
	Out of his charity, who being then appointed	
	Master of this design, did give us, with	

---

144. **bark:** small sailing vessel
146. **carcass of a butt:** tub of a wine cask

Rich garments, linen, stuffs, and necessaries,
Which since have steaded much. So, of his gentleness,
Knowing I lov'd my books, he furnish'd me
From mine own library with volumes that
I prize above my dukedom.

Miranda   Would I might
But ever see that man!

Prospero   Now I arise.   *Resumes his mantle*
Sit still, and hear the last of our sea-sorrow.   170
Here in this island we arriv'd, and here
Have I, thy schoolmaster, made thee more profit
Than other princes can, that have more time
For vainer hours, and tutors not so careful.

Miranda   Heavens thank you for't! And now, I pray you, sir,
For still 'tis beating in my mind, your reason
For raising this sea-storm?

Prospero   Know thus far forth.
By accident most strange, bountiful Fortune,
Now my dear lady, hath mine enemies
Brought to this shore; and by my prescience   180
I find my zenith doth depend upon
A most auspicious star, whose influence
If now I court not, but omit, my fortunes
Will ever after droop. Here cease more questions.
Thou art inclin'd to sleep. 'Tis a good dulness,
And give it way. I know thou canst not choose.

Miranda sleeps   [Scene 3]

Come away, servant, come! I am ready now.
Approach, my Ariel! Come!

Enter Ariel

Ariel   All hail, great master! Grave sir, hail! I come
To answer thy best pleasure; be't to fly,   190
To swim, to dive into the fire, to ride
On the curl'd clouds. To thy strong bidding, task
Ariel, and all his quality.

Prospero   Hast thou, spirit,

---

180. **prescience:** foreknowledge

23

	Perform'd to point the tempest that I bade thee!
Ariel	To every article.
	I boarded the King's ship. Now on the beak,
	Now in the waist, the deck, in every cabin
	I flam'd amazement. Sometime I'd divide
	And burn in many places; on the topmast,
	The yards and bowsprit, would I flame distinctly,
	Then meet and join. Jove's lightning, the precursors
	O' th' dreadful thunder-claps, more momentary
	And sight-outrunning were not. The fire, and cracks
	of sulphurous roaring, the most mighty Neptune
	Seem to besiege, and make his bold waves tremble,
	Yea, his dread trident shake.
Prospero	My brave spirit!
	Who was so firm, so constant, that this coil
	Would not infect his reason?
Ariel	Not a soul
	But felt a fever of the mad, and play'd
	Some tricks of desperation. All but mariners
	Plung'd in the foaming brine, and quit the vessel,
	Then all afire with me. The King's son, Ferdinand,
	With hair up-staring – then like reeds, not hair –
	Was the first man that leap'd; cried, 'Hell is empty,
	And all the devils are here!'
Prospero	Why, that's my spirit!
	But was not this nigh shore?
Ariel	Close by, my master.
Prospero	But are they, Ariel, safe?
Ariel	Not a hair perish'd;
	On their sustaining garments not a blemish,
	But fresher than before: and as thou bad'st me
	In troops I have dispers'd them 'bout the isle!
	The King's son have I landed by himself,
	Whom I left cooling of the air with sighs
	In an odd angle of the isle, and sitting
	His arms in this sad knot.
Prospero	Of the King's ship,
	The mariners, say how thou hast dispos'd,
	And all the rest o' the fleet?
Ariel	Safely in the harbour
	Is the King's ship, in the deep nook where once

200

210

220

---

207. **coil:** noisy disturbance
216. **nigh:** near

Thou call'dst me up at midnight to fetch dew
From the still-vex'd Bermoothes, there she's hid;
The mariners all under hatches stow'd,   230
Who, with a charm join'd to their suffer'd labour,
I have left asleep. And for the rest o' the fleet,
Which I dispers'd, they all have met again,
And are upon the Mediterranean flote
Bound sadly home for Naples,
Supposing that they saw the King's ship wreck'd,
And his great person perish.

Prospero   Ariel, thy charge
Exactly is perform'd; but there's more work.
What is the time o' the day?

Ariel   Past the mid season.

Prospero At least two glasses. The time 'twixt six and now   240
Must by us both be spent most preciously.

Ariel   Is there more toil? Since thou dost give me pains,
Let me remember thee what thou hast promis'd,
Which is not yet perform'd me.

Prospero   How now? Moody?
What is't thou canst demand?

Ariel   My liberty.

Prospero Before the time be out? No more!

Ariel   I prithee,
Remember I have done thee worthy service,
Told thee no lies, made thee no mistakings, serv'd   [248]
Without or grudge, or grumblings. Thou didst promise
To bate me a full year.

Prospero   Dost thou forget   250
From what a torment I did free thee?

Ariel   No.

Prospero Thou dost, and think'st it much to tread the ooze
Of the salt deep,
To run upon the sharp wind of the north,
To do me business in the veins o' th' earth
When it is bak'd with frost.

Ariel   I do not, sir.

Prospero Thou liest, malignant thing! Hast thou forgot
The foul witch Sycorax, who with age and envy
Was grown into a hoop? Hast thou forgot her?

Ariel   No, sir.

---

229. **Bermoothes:** the Bermudas
234. **flote:** sea
250. **bate me:** shorten my term of service

Prospero and Ariel

Prospero	Thou hast! Where was she born? Speak! Tell me!	260
Ariel	Sir, in Argier.	
Prospero	O, was she so? I must	[261]

Once in a month recount what you hast been,
Which thou forget'st. This damn'd witch Sycorax,
For mischiefs manifold, and sorceries terrible
To enter human hearing, from Argier   [265]
Thou know'st was banish'd. For one thing she did
They would not take her life. Is not this true?

Ariel   Ay, sir.

Prospero This blue-eyed hag was hither brought with child,
And here was left by the sailors. Thou my slave,   270
As thou report'st thyself, was then her servant;
And for thou wast a spirit too delicate
To act her earthy and abhorr'd commands,
Refusing her grand hests, she did confine thee,
By help of her more potent ministers,
And in her most unmitigable rage,
Into a cloven pine, within which rift
Imprison'd, thou didst painfully remain
A dozen years: within which space she died,
And left thee there, where thou didst vent thy groans   280
As fast as mill-wheels strike. Then was this island –
Save for the son, that she did litter here,
A freckled whelp, hag-born – not honour'd with
A human shape.

Ariel   Yes, Caliban her son.

Prospero Dull thing, I say so! He, that Caliban
Whom now I keep in service. Thou best know'st
What torment I did find thee in; thy groans
Did make wolves howl, and penetrate the breasts
Of ever-angry bears. It was a torment
To lay upon the damn'd, which Sycorax   290
Could not again undo. It was mine art,
When I arriv'd and heard thee, that made gape
The pine, and let thee out.

Ariel   I thank thee, master.

Prospero If thou more murmur'st, I will rend an oak
And peg thee in his knotty entrails, till
Thou has howl'd away twelve winters.

---

261.   **Argier:** Algiers

Ariel   Pardon, master,
            I will be correspondent to command
            And do my spiriting gently.
Prospero   Do so, and after two days
            I will discharge thee.
Ariel   That's my noble master!
            What shall I do? Say what; what shall I do?   300

Prospero Go make thyself like a nymph o' the sea,
            Be subject to no sight but thine and mine, invisible
            To every eyeball else. Go take this shape
            And hither come in't. Go! Hence with diligence!

                                              Exit Ariel   [Scene 4]

            Awake, dear heart, awake, thou hast slept well;
            Awake!
Miranda   The strangeness of your story put
            Heaviness in me.
Prospero   Shake it off. Come on,
            We'll visit Caliban, my slave, who never
            Yields us kind answer.
Miranda   'Tis a villain, sir,
            I do not love to look on.
Prospero   But, as 'tis,   310
            We cannot miss him. He does make our fire,
            Fetch in our wood, and serves in offices
            That profit us. What, ho! Slave! Caliban!
            Thou earth, thou! Speak!
Caliban   (*within*) There's wood enough within.
Prospero Come forth, I say! There's other business for thee.
            Come, thou tortoise! When?

Re-enter Ariel like a water-nymph

            Fine apparition! My quaint Ariel,
            Hark in thine ear.
Ariel   My lord, it shall be done.   *Exit*
Prospero Thou poisonous slave, got by the devil himself
            Upon thy wicked dam, come forth!   320

---

297. **correspondent:** obedient
320. **dam:** female parent

THE TERRIBLE SHAPE —
— CALIBAN —

Enter Caliban

Caliban	As wicked dew as e'er my mother brush'd
	With raven's feather from unwholesome fen
	Drop on you both! A south-west blow on ye
	And blister you all o'er!
Prospero	For this, be sure, to-night thou shalt have cramps,
	Side-stitches, that shall pen thy breath up; urchins
	Shall, for that vast of night that they may work,
	All exercise on thee; thou shalt be pinch'd
	As thick as honeycomb, each pinch more stinging
	Than bees that made 'em.

Caliban   I must eat my dinner.   330
This island's mine, by Sycorax my mother,
Which thou tak'st from me. When thou camest first,
Thou strok'st me, and made much of me, wouldst
     give me
Water with berries in 't, and teach me how
To name the bigger light, and how the less,
That burn by day, and night. And then I lov'd thee,
And show'd thee all the qualities o' th' isle,
The fresh springs, brine-pits, barren place and fertile.
Curs'd be that I did so! All the charms
Of Sycorax, toads, beetles, bats, light on you!   340
For I am all the subjects that you have,
Which first was mine own king: and here you sty me
In this hard rock, whiles you do keep from me
The rest o' th' island.

Prospero   Thou most lying slave,
Whom stripes may move, not kindness! I have us'd thee
Filth as thou art, with human care, and lodg'd thee
In mine own cell, till thou didst seek to violate
The honour of my child.

Caliban   O ho, O ho! Would't have been done!
Thou didst prevent me. I had peopled else   350
This isle with Calibans.

Miranda   Abhorred slave,   [351]
Which any print of goodness wilt not take,
Being capable of all ill! I pitied thee,
Took pains to make thee speak, taught thee each hour

---

326. **urchins:** hedgehogs

345. **stripes:** lashes

One thing or other. When thou didst not, savage,
Know thine own meaning, but wouldst gabble like
A thing most brutish, I endow'd thy purposes
With words that make them known. But thy vile race,
Though thou didst learn, had that in't which good
  natures
Could not abide to be with; therefore wast thou   360
Deservedly confin'd into this rock, who hadst
Deserv'd more than a prison.

Caliban   You taught me language, and my profit on't
Is, I know how to curse. The red plague rid you
For learning me your language!

Prospero   Hag-seed, hence!
Fetch us in fuel, and be quick, thou 'rt best
To answer other business. Shrug'st thou, malice?
If thou neglect'st, or dost unwillingly
What I command, I'll rack thee with old cramps,
Fill all thy bones with aches, make thee roar,   370
That beasts shall tremble at thy din.

Caliban   No, pray thee!
(*aside*) I must obey, his art is of such power,
It would control my dam's god Setebos,
And make a vassal of him.

Prospero   So, slave. Hence!   *Exit Caliban*

Re-enter Ariel, invisible, playing and singing;
Ferdinand following

ARIEL'S SONG   [Scene 5]

Come unto these yellow sands,
  And then take hands:
Courtsied when you have, and kiss'd
  The wild waves whist:
Foot it featly here and there;
  And, sweet sprites, the burthen bear   380
Hark, hark!
Burthen (dispersedly). Bow-wow.
The watch dogs bark:
Burthen (dispersedly). Bow-wow.
Hark, hark! I hear

---

374. **vassal:** manservant

31

The strain of strutting chanticleer
Cry, Cock-a-diddle-dow.
Ferdinand Where should this music be? I' th' air, or th' earth?
It sounds no more: and sure it waits upon
Some god o' th' island. Sitting on a bank,
Weeping again the King my father's wreck.
This music crept by me upon the waters,   390
Allaying both their fury and my passion
With its sweet air. Thence I have follow'd it,
Or it hath drawn me rather. But 'tis gone.
No, it begins again.
Ariel sings

Full fathom five thy father lies,
    Of his bones are coral made:
Those are pearls that were his eyes,
    Nothing of him that doth fade,
But doth suffer a sea-change
    Into something rich, and strange.   400
Sea-nymphs hourly ring his knell:
                                    Burthen. Ding-dong.
Ariel   Hark! Now I hear them – Ding-dong, bell.
Ferdinand The ditty does remember my drown'd father.
This is no mortal business, nor no sound
That the earth owes – I hear it now above me.
Prospero The fringed curtains of thine eye advance,
And say what thou seest yond.
Miranda   What is't? A spirit?
Lord, how it looks about! Believe me, sir,
It carries a brave form. But 'tis a spirit.   410
Prospero No, wench. It eats and sleeps and hath such senses
As we have, such. This gallant which thou seest
Was in the wreck; and, but he's something stain'd
With grief that's beauty's canker, thou mightest
    call him
A goodly person. He hath lost his fellows,
And strays about to find 'em.
Miranda   I might call him
A thing divine, for nothing natural
I ever saw so noble.

---

384. **chanticleer:** rooster   **Ferdinand, Miranda, and Prospero ▶**
406. **owes:** owns
413. **but:** except that

Prospero	(*aside*) It goes on, I see,
	As my soul prompts it. Spirit, fine spirit, I'll free thee
	Within two days for this!
Ferdinand	Most sure the goddess	420
	On whom these airs attend! Vouchsafe my prayer
	May know if you remain upon this island,
	And that you will some good instruction give
	How I may bear me here. My prime request
	Which I do last pronounce is – O you wonder! –
	If you be maid, or no?
Miranda	No wonder, sir,
	But certainly a maid.
Ferdinand	My language! Heavens!
	I am the best of them that speak this speech,
	Were I but where 'tis spoken.
Prospero	How? The best?
	What were thou, if the King of Naples heard thee?	430
Ferdinand	A single thing, as I am now, that wonders
	To hear thee speak of Naples. He does hear me,
	And that he does, I weep. Myself am Naples,
	Who with mine eyes, never since at ebb, beheld
	The King my father wreck'd.
Miranda	Alack for mercy!
Ferdinand	Yes, faith, and all his lords, the Duke of Milan
	And his brave son being twain.
Prospero	(*aside*) The Duke of Milan,
	And his more braver daughter could control thee,
	If now 'twere fit to do't. At the first sight
	They have chang'd eyes. Delicate Ariel,	440
	I'll set thee free for this. (*to Ferdinand*) A word, good sir.
	I fear you have done yourself some wrong. A word!
Miranda	Why speaks my father so ungently? This
	Is the third man that e'er I saw; the first
	That e'er I sigh'd for. Pity move my father
	To be inclin'd my way!
Ferdinand	O, if a virgin,
	And your affection not gone forth, I'll make you
	The Queen of Naples.
Prospero	Soft, sir! One word more.

---

431. **single:** poor

(*aside*) They are both in either's powers. But this
  swift business
I must uneasy make, lest too light winning   450
Make the prize light. (*to Ferdinand*) One word more!
  I charge thee
That thou attend me. Thou dost here usurp
The name thou ow'st not, and hast put thyself
Upon this island as a spy, to win it
From me, the lord on 't.

Ferdinand   No, as I am a man!

Miranda There's nothing ill can dwell in such a temple.
If the ill spirit have so fair a house,
Good things will strive to dwell with't.

Prospero   Follow me.
Speak not you for him. He's a traitor. Come!   460
I'll manacle thy neck and feet together.
Sea-water salt thou drink; thy food shall be
The fresh-brook mussels, wither'd roots, and husks
Wherein the acorn cradled. Follow!

Ferdinand   No!
I will resist such entertainment till
Mine enemy has more power.

He draws, and is charmed from moving

Miranda   O dear father,
Make not too rash a trial of him, for
He's gentle, and not fearful.

Prospero   What! I say,
My foot my tutor? Put thy sword up, traitor,
Who mak'st a show, but dar'st not strike, thy conscience 470
Is so possess'd with guilt. Come, from thy ward!
For I can here disarm thee with this stick,
And make thy weapon drop.

Miranda   Beseech you, father!

Prospero Hence! Hang not on my garments.

Miranda   Sir, have pity.
I'll be his surety.

Prospero   Silence! one word more

---

452. **usurp:** falsely assume
471. **ward:** defensive posture

          Shall make me chide thee, if not hate thee. What?
          An advocate for an imposter? Hush!   [477]
          Thou think'st there is no more such shapes as he,
          Having seen but him and Caliban. Foolish wench!
          To th' most of men this is a Caliban,   480
          And they to him are angels.

Miranda   My affections
          Are then most humble. I have no ambition
          To see a goodlier man.

Prospero   Come on, obey!
          Thy nerves are in their infancy again,
          And have no vigour in them.

Ferdinand   So they are.
          My spirits, as in a dream, are all bound up.
          My father's loss, the weakness which I feel,
          The wreck of all my friends, nor this man's threats,
          To whom I am subdued, are but light to me,
          Might I but through my prison once a day   490
          Behold this maid, all corners else o' th' earth
          Let liberty make use of. Space enough
          Have I in such a prison.

Prospero   (*aside*) It works. (*to Ferdinand*) Come on.
          Thou hast done well, fine Ariel! (*to Ferdinand*) Follow me.
          (*to Ariel.*) Hark what thou else shalt do me.

Miranda   Be of comfort.
          My father's of a better nature, sir,
          Than he appears by 's speech: This is unwonted
          Which now came from him.

Prospero   Thou shalt be as free
          As mountain winds; but then exactly do
          All points of my command.

Ariel   To th'syllable.   500

Prospero   Come, follow! Speak not for him.   *Exeunt*   [501]

Act Second

Scene 1 [Scene 6]

Another part of the island

Enter Alonso, Sebastian, Antonio, Gonzalo,
Adrian, Francisco, and others   [0]

Gonzalo	Beseech you, sir, be merry. You have cause,
	So have we all, of joy; for our escape
	Is much beyond our loss. Our hint of woe
	Is common. Every day some sailor's wife,
	The masters of some merchant, and the merchant,
	Have just our theme of woe; but for the miracle,
	I mean our preservation, few in millions
	Can speak like us. Then wisely, good sir, weigh
	Our sorrow with our comfort.
Alonso	Prithee, peace.
Sebastian	He receives comfort like cold porridge. 10
Antonio	The visitor will not give him o'er so.
Sebastian	Look, he's winding up the watch of his wit, by and
	by it will strike.
Gonzalo	Sir, –
Sebastian	One: tell.
Gonzalo	When every grief is entertain'd that's offer'd,
	Comes to th' entertainer –
Sebastian	A dollar.
Gonzalo	Dolour comes to him indeed. You have spoken truer
	than you purpos'd. 20

---

3. **hint:** prompting
18. **dollar:** English name for German *thaler*
19. **dolour:** suffering

Sebastian	You have taken it wiselier than I meant you should.
Gonzalo	Therefore, my lord, –
Antonio	Fie, what a spendthrift is he of his tongue!
Alonso	I prithee spare.
Gonzalo	Well, I have done. But yet, –
Sebastian	He will be talking.
Antonio	Which, of he or Adrian, for a good wager, first begins to crow?
Sebastian	The old cock.
Antonio	The cockerel.
Sebastian	Done. The wager?
Antonio	A laughter.
Sebastian	A match!
Adrian	Though this island seem to be desert, –
Sebastian	Ha, ha, ha! – So, you're paid.
Adrian	Uninhabitable, and almost inaccessible, –
Sebastian	Yet, –
Adrian	Yet, –
Antonio	He could not miss't.
Adrian	It must needs be of subtle, tender and delicate temperance.
Antonio	Temperance was a delicate wench.
Sebastian	Ay, and a subtle, as he most learnedly deliver'd.
Adrian	The air breathes upon us here most sweetly.
Sebastian	As if it had lungs, and rotten ones.
Antonio	Or, as 'twere perfum'd by a fen.
Gonzalo	Here is everything advantageous to life.
Antonio	True, save means to live.
Sebastian	Of that there's none, or little.
Gonzalo	How lush and lusty the grass looks! How green!
Antonio	The ground, indeed, is tawny.
Sebastian	With an eye of green in't.
Antonio	He misses not much.
Sebastian	No, he doth but mistake the truth totally.
Gonzalo	But the rarity of it is, which is indeed almost beyond credit, –
Sebastian	As many vouch'd rarities are.
Gonzalo	That our garments, being, as they were, drench'd in the sea, hold notwithstanding, their freshness and glosses, being rather new-dyed than stain'd with salt water.

Line numbers: 30, [35], 40, 50, 60

41. **temperance:** climate

46. **fen:** swamp

Richard Curnock as Alonso; Peter Waisberg as Adrian

Antonio	If but one of his pockets could speak, would it not say he lies?	[62-64]
Sebastian	Ay, or very falsely pocket up his report.	
Gonzalo	Methinks our garments are now as fresh as when we put them on first in Afric, at the marriage of the King's fair daughter Claribel to the King of Tunis.	
Sebastian	'Twas a sweet marriage, and we prosper well in our return.	
Adrian	Tunis was never grac'd before with such a paragon to their queen.	70
Gonzalo	Not since widow Dido's time.	
Antonio	Widow? A pox o' that! How came that widow in? Widow Dido!	
Sebastian	What if he had said 'widower Æneas' too? Good Lord, how you take it!	
Adrian	'Widow Dido' said you? You make me study of that. She was of Carthage, not of Tunis.	
Gonzalo	This Tunis, sir, was Carthage	
Adrian	Carthage?	80
Gonzalo	I assure you, Carthage.	
Antonio	His word is more than the miraculous harp.	[82-83]
Sebastian	He hath rais'd the wall, and houses too.	
Antonio	What impossible matter will he make easy next?	
Sebastian	I think he will carry this island home in his pocket, and give it his son for an apple.	[85-90]
Antonio	And sowing the kernels of it in the sea, bring forth more islands.	
Gonzalo	Ay.	
Antonio	Why, in good time.	90
Gonzalo	Sir, we were talking, that our garments seem now as fresh as when we were at Tunis at the marriage of your daughter, who is now Queen.	
Antonio	And the rarest that e'er came there.	
Sebastian	Bate, I beseech you, widow Dido.	[95]
Antonio	O, widow Dido? Ay, widow Dido.	
Gonzalo	Is not, sir, my doublet as fresh as the first day I wore it? I mean, in a sort.	
Antonio	That sort was well fish'd for.	
Gonzalo	When I wore it at your daughter's marriage?	100
Alonso	You cram these words into mine ears against	

The stomach of my sense. Would I had never
Married my daughter there! For, coming thence,
My son is lost, and, in my rate, she too,
Who is so far from Italy remov'd
I ne'er again shall see her. O thou mine heir
Of Naples and of Milan, what strange fish
Hath made his meal on thee?

Francisco   Sir, he may live.   [108]
I saw him beat the surges under him,
And ride upon their backs. He trod the water,   110
Whose enmity he flung aside, and breasted
The surge most swoln that met him. His bold head   [112]
'Bove the contentious waves he kept, and oar'd
Himself with his good arms in lusty stroke
To th' shore, that o'er his wave-worn basis bow'd,
As stooping to relieve him. I not doubt
He came alive to land.

Alonso   No, no, he's gone.

Sebastian Sir, you may thank yourself for this great loss,
That would not bless our Europe with your daughter,
But rather lose her to an African,   120
Where she, at least, is banish'd from your eye,   [121-22]
Who hath cause to wet the grief on 't.

Alonso   Prithee peace.

Sebastian You were kneel'd to and importun'd otherwise
By all of us; and the fair soul herself   [125-27]
Weigh'd between loathness and obedience, at
Which end o' the beam should bow. We have lost
    your son,
I fear for ever. Milan and Naples have
More widows in them of this business' making
Than we bring men to comfort them.
The fault's your own.

Alonso   So is the dear'st o' the loss.   130

Gonzalo My lord Sebastian,
The truth you speak doth lack some gentleness,
And time to speak it in. You rub the sore,
When you should bring the plaster.

Sebastian   Very well.

Antonio And most chirurgeonly.   [135]

---

109.   **surges:** great waves
124.   **importun'd:** petitioned

41

Gonzalo	It is foul weather in us all, good sir.
	When you are cloudy.
Sebastian	Foul weather?
Antonio	Very foul.
Gonzalo	Had I plantation of this isle, my lord, –
Antonio	He'ld sow't with nettle-seed.
Sebastian	Or docks, or mallows.
Gonzalo	And were the King on't, what would I do?
Sebastian	'Scape being drunk for want of wine.
Gonzalo	I' th' commonwealth I would by contraries

Gonzalo: (continued)
Execute all things. For no kind of traffic
Would I admit, no name of magistrate.
Letters should not be known. Riches, poverty,
And use of service, none. Contract, succession,
Bourn, bound of land, tilth, vineyard, none.
No use of metal, corn, or wine, or oil.
No occupation, all men idle, all,
And women too, but innocent and pure.
No sovereignty –

Sebastian: Yet he would be king on 't.

Antonio: The latter end of his commonwealth forgets the
beginning.

Gonzalo: All things in common nature should produce
Without sweat or endeavour. Treason, felony,
Sword, pike, knife, gun, or need of any engine
Would I not have; but nature should bring forth
Of its own kind, all foison, all abundance,
To feed my innocent people.

Sebastian: No marrying 'mong his subjects?

Antonio: None, man, all idle; whores and knaves.

Gonzalo: I would with such perfection govern, sir,
To excel the Golden Age.

Sebastian: 'Save his majesty!

Antonio: Long live Gonzalo!

Gonzalo: And, – do you mark me sir?

Alonso: Prithee no more. Thou dost talk nothing to me.

Gonzalo: I do well believe your highness, and did it to
minister occasion to these gentlemen, who are of
such sensible and nimble lungs that they always use
to laugh at nothing.

140

150

160

137.	**cloudy:** sullen		147.	**Bourn:** private property limits
143.	**traffic:** buying and selling		156.	**engine:** trickery
146.	**service:** servant class		158.	**foison:** plentiful crop
146.	**succession:** inheritance		167.	**minister occasion:** provide opportunity

Antonio	'Twas you we laugh'd at.	170
Gonzalo	Who, in this kind of merry fooling am nothing to you, so you may continue, and laugh at nothing still.	
Antonio	What a blow was there given!	
Sebastian	And it had not fallen flat-long.	
Gonzalo	You are gentlemen of brave mettle. You would lift the moon out of her sphere, if she would continue in it five weeks without changing.	

Enter Ariel (invisible) playing solemn music

Sebastian	We would so, and then go a bat-fowling.	
Antonio	Nay, good my lord, be not angry.	180
Gonzalo	No, I warrant you, I will not adventure my discretion so weakly. Will you laugh me asleep, for I am very heavy?	
Antonio	Go sleep, and hear us.	

All sleep except Alonso, Sebastian, and Antonio [Scene 7]

Alonso	What, all so soon asleep? I wish mine eyes Would, with themselves, shut up my thoughts. I find They are inclin'd to do so.	
Sebastian	Please you, sir, Do not omit the heavy offer of it. It seldom visits sorrow; when it doth, It is a comforter.	
Antonio	We two, my lord, Will guard your person while you take your rest, And watch your safety.	190
Alonso	Thank you. – Wondrous heavy.	

Alonso sleeps. Exit Ariel

Sebastian	What a strange drowsiness possesses them!	
Antonio	It is the quality o' the climate.	
Sebastian	Why Doth it not then our eyelids sink? I find not Myself dispos'd to sleep.	

175. **flat-long:** hit with the flat of a sword

179. **bat-fowling:** hunting birds at night with a stick

Antonio	Nor I. My spirits are nimble.

They fell together all, as by consent
They dropp'd, as by a thunder-stroke. What might,
Worthy Sebastian? – O what might? – No more!
And yet, methinks I see it in thy face,⁣   200
What thou shouldst be. The occasion speaks thee, and
My strong imagination sees a crown
Dropping upon thy head.

Sebastian   What? Art thou waking?

Antonio Do you not hear me speak?

Sebastian   I do, and surely
It is a sleepy language, and thou speak'st
Out of thy sleep. What is it thou didst say?
This is a strange repose, to be asleep
With eyes wide open; standing, speaking, moving.
And yet so fast asleep.

Antonio   Noble Sebastian,
Thou let'st thy fortune sleep – die, rather; wink'st   210
Whiles thou art waking.

Sebastian   Thou dost snore distinctly.
There's meaning in thy snores.

Antonio I am more serious than my custom. You
Must be so too, if heed me; which to do
Trebles thee o'er.

Sebastian   Well, I am standing water.

Antonio I'll teach you how to flow.

Sebastian   Do so: to ebb
Hereditary sloth instructs me.

Antonio   O,
If you but knew how you the purpose cherish
Whiles thus you mock it! How, in stripping it,   [219-20]
You more invest it! Ebbing men, indeed,
Most often do so near the bottom run
By their own fear, or sloth.

Sebastian   Prithee say on.
The setting of thine eyes and cheek proclaim   [223-25]
A matter from thee; and a birth, indeed,
Which throes thee much to yield.

Antonio   Thus, sir:
Although this lord of weak remembrance, this,

---

201. **speaks:** speaks to
210. **wink'st:** sleep
215. **trebles thee:** makes you three times greater

Antonio (standing) with Alonso, Adrian, and Gonzalo, played by Lewis Gordon

Who shall be of as little memory
When he is earth'd, hath here almost persuaded –
For he's a spirit of persuasion, only   [229-30]
Professes to persuade the King his son's alive,
'Tis as impossible that he's undrown'd
As he that sleeps here swims.

Sebastian   I have no hope
That he's undrown'd.

Antonio   O, out of that 'no hope'
What great hope have you! No hope that way is   [234-37]
Another way so high a hope that even
Ambition cannot pierce a wink beyond,
But doubt discovery there. Will you grant with me
That Ferdinand is drown'd?

Sebastian   He's gone.

Antonio   Then, tell me,
Who's the next heir of Naples?

Sebastian   Claribel.

Antonio   She that is Queen of Tunis; she that dwells   240
Ten leagues beyond man's life; she that from Naples
Can have no note, unless the sun were post, –
The man i' the moon's too slow, – till new-born chin
Be rough and razorable; she that from whom
We all were sea-swallow'd, though some cast again,
And, by that destiny, to perform an act
Whereof what's past is prologue, what to come,
In yours and my discharge.

Sebastian   What stuff is this? How say you?
'Tis true, my brother's daughter's Queen of Tunis;
So is she heir of Naples, 'twixt which regions   250
There is some space.

Antonio   A space whose every cubit
Seems to cry out, 'How shall that Claribel
Measure us back to Naples? Keep in Tunis,
And let Sebastian wake.' Say this were death
That now hath seiz'd them, why, they were no worse
Than now they are. There be that can rule Naples
As well as he that sleeps; lords that can prate
As amply and unnecessarily
As this Gonzalo. I myself could make

---

228. **earth'd:** buried

A chough of as deep chat. O, that you bore   260
The mind that I do! What a sleep were this
For your advancement! Do you understand me?

Sebastian Methinks I do.

Antonio   And how does your content
Tender your own good fortune?

Sebastian   I remember
You did supplant your brother Prospero.

Antonio   True.
And look how well my garments sit upon me,
Much feater than before. My brother's servants
Were then my fellows. Now they are my men.

Sebastian But for your conscience?

Antonio Ay, sir, where lies that? If 'twere a kibe,   270
'Twould put me to my slipper, but I feel not
This deity in my bosom. Twenty consciences,
That stand 'twixt me, and Milan, candied be they,
And melt ere they molest! Here lies your brother,
No better than the earth he lies upon,
If he were that which now he's like, that's dead,
Whom I, with this obedient steel, three inches of it,
Can lay to bed for ever; whiles you, doing thus,
To the perpetual wink for aye might put
This ancient morsel, this Sir Prudence, who   280
Should not upbraid our course. For all the rest,
They'll take suggestion, as a cat laps milk,
They'll tell the clock to any business that
We say befits the hour.

Sebastian   Thy case, dear friend,
Shall be my precedent. As thou got'st Milan,
I'll come by Naples. Draw thy sword. One stroke
Shall free thee from the tribute which thou payest,
And I the King shall love thee.

Antonio   Draw together,
And when I rear my hand, do you the like,
To fall it on Gonzalo.

Sebastian   O, but one word.   *They talk apart*   290

Re-enter Ariel, invisible   [Scene 8]

---

260. **chough:** a chattering bird   270. **kibe:** chilblain   281. **upbraid:** censure
267. **feater:** more suitable   273. **candied:** frozen   283. **tell the clock:** agree to

Ariel   My master through his art foresees the danger
            That you, his friend, are in, and sends me forth,
            For else his project dies, to keep them living.

Sings in Gonzalo's ear

                While you here do snoring lie,
                Open-eyed conspiracy
                    His time doth take.
                If of life you keep a care,
                Shake off slumber and beware:
                    Awake, awake!
Antonio   Then let us both be sudden.
Gonzalo   Now, good angels   300
            Preserve the King!   *They wake*
Alonso   Why, how now? Ho, awake! – Why are you drawn?
            Wherefore this ghastly looking?
Gonzalo   What's the matter?
Sebastian Whiles we stood here securing your repose,
            Even now, we heard a hollow burst of bellowing
            Like bulls, or rather lions. Did't not wake you?
            It struck mine ear most terribly.
Alonso   I heard nothing.
Antonio   O, 'twas a din to fright a monster's ear,
            To make an earthquake! Sure, it was the roar
            Of a whole herd of lions.
Alonso   Heard you this, Gonzalo?   310
Gonzalo   Upon mine honour, sir, I heard a humming,
            And that a strange one too, which did awake me.
            I shak'd you, sir, and cried. As mine eyes open'd,
            I saw their weapons drawn, – there was a noise,
            That's verily. 'Tis best we stand upon our guard,
            Or that we quit this place. Let's draw our weapons.
Alonso   Lead off this ground and let's make further search
            For my poor son.
Gonzalo   Heavens keep him from these beasts!
            For he is sure i' th' island.
Alonso   Lead away.
Ariel   Prospero my lord shall know what I have done.   320
            So, King, go safely on to seek thy son.   *Exeunt*

---

315.   **verily:** true

Scene 2

Another part of the island

Enter Caliban with a burden of wood. A noise of thunder heard

Caliban All the infections that the sun sucks up
From bogs, fens, flats, on Prosper fall, and make him
By inch-meal a disease! His spirits hear me,
And yet I needs must curse. But they'll nor pinch,
Fright me with urchin-shows, pitch me i' the mire,
Nor lead me, like a firebrand, in the dark
Out of my way, unless he bid 'em. But
For every trifle are they set upon me,
Sometime like apes, that mow and chatter at me,
And after bite me, then like hedgehogs, which   10
Lie tumbling in my barefoot way, and mount
Their pricks at my footfall; sometime am I
All wound with adders, who with cloven tongues
Do hiss me into madness.

Enter Trinculo

                        Lo, now, lo!
Here comes a spirit of his, and to torment me
For bringing wood in slowly. I'll fall flat,
Perchance he will not mind me.

Trinculo Here's neither bush nor shrub, to bear off any
weather at all, and another storm brewing. I hear
it sing i' the wind. Yond same black cloud, yond   20
huge one, looks like a foul bombard that would shed
his liquor. If it should thunder as it did before,
I know not where to hide my head. Yond same cloud
cannot choose but fall by pailfuls. What have we
here? A man, or a fish? Dead or alive? A fish! He
smells like a fish; a very ancient and fish-like smell;
a kind of, not of the newest Poor-John. A strange

---

3. **inch-meal:** inch by inch   21. **bombard:** large leather vessel

9. **mow:** make faces   27. **Poor-John:** fish that resembles a cod

fish! Were I in England now, as once I was, and
had but this fish painted, not a holiday fool there
but would give a piece of silver. There would this   30
monster make a man. Any strange beast there makes
a man. When they will not give a doit to relieve a   [32]
lame beggar, they will lay out ten to see a dead Indian.
Legg'd like a man! And his fins like arms. Warm o'
my troth! I do now let loose my opinion, hold it
no longer. This is no fish, but an islander, that hath
lately suffered by a thunderbolt. (*Thunder.*) Alas, the
storm is come again! My best way is to creep under
his gaberdine. There is no other shelter hereabout.
Misery acquaints a man with strange bed-fellows.   40
I will here shroud till the dregs of the storm be past.

Enter Stephano, singing: a bottle in his hand

Stephano   I shall no more to sea, to sea,
                    Here shall I die a-shore, –
        This is a very scurvy tune to sing at a man's funeral.
        Well, here's my comfort.   *Drinks*
        (*sings*)
                    The master, the swabber, the boatswain, and I,
                    The gunner, and his mate,
                    Lov'd Mall, Meg, and Marian, and Margery,
                    But none of us car'd for Kate.
                    For she had a tongue with a tang,   50
                    Would cry to a sailor, Go hang!
                    She lov'd not the savour of tar nor of pitch,
                    Yet a tailor might scratch her where'er she did itch.
                    Then, to sea, boys, and let her go hang!
        This is a scurvy tune too. But here's my comfort.
                                     Drinks
Caliban   Do not torment me! – O!
Stephano   What's the matter? Have we devils here? Do
you put tricks upon 's with savages, and men of Ind,
ha? I have not scap'd drowning, to be afeard now
of your four legs. For it hath been said, 'As proper a   60
man as ever went on four legs cannot make him give

32. **doit:** small coin
39. **gaberdine:** cloak

ground'; and it shall be said so again, while Stephano
breathes at nostrils.

Caliban The spirit torments me! – O!

Stephano This is some monster of the isle with four legs, who
hath got, as I take it, an ague. Where the devil
should he learn our language? I will give him
some relief, if it be but for that. If I can recover
him, and keep him tame, and get to Naples with
him, he's a present for any emperor that ever trod   70
on neat's-leather!

Caliban Do not torment me, prithee! I'll bring my wood
home faster.

Stephano He's in his fit now, and does not talk after the
wisest. He shall taste of my bottle. If he have
never drunk wine afore, it will go near to remove
his fit. If I can recover him, and keep him tame, I
will not take too much for him. He shall pay for
him that hath him, and that soundly.

Caliban Thou dost me yet but little hurt. Thou wilt anon, I   80
know it by thy trembling. Now Prosper works
upon thee.

Stephano Come on your ways. Open your mouth. Here is
that which will give language to you, cat. Open
your mouth. This will shake your shaking, I can
tell you, and that soundly. You cannot tell who's
your friend. Open your chaps again.

Trinculo I should know that voice! It should be – but he is
drown'd, and these are devils. – O defend me!

Stephano Four legs and two voices – a most delicate monster!   90
His forward voice, now, is to speak well of his
friend. His backward voice is to utter foul speeches,
and to detract. If all the wine in my bottle will
recover him, I will help his ague. Come! – Amen!
I will pour some in thy other mouth.

Trinculo Stephano!

Stephano Doth thy other mouth call me? Mercy, mercy!
This is a devil, and no monster. I will leave him,
I have no long spoon.

Trinculo Stephano! If thou beest Stephano, touch me, and   100

---

66. **ague:** fever

71. **neat's-leather:** cowhide

99. **long spoon:** referring to the adage "He who sups
with the devil must have a long spoon."

	speak to me; for I am Trinculo, be not afeard,
	thy good friend Trinculo.
Stephano	If thou beest Trinculo, come forth. I'll pull thee
	by the lesser legs. If any be Trinculo's legs, these
	are they. Thou art very Trinculo indeed! How
	cam'st thou to be the siege of this moon-calf? Can [106]
	he vent Trinculos?
Trinculo	I took him to be killed with a thunder-stroke. But
	art thou not drown'd, Stephano? I hope, now,
	thou art not drown'd. Is the storm overblown? 110
	I hid me under the dead moon-calf's gaberdine, for
	fear of the storm. And art thou living, Stephano?
	O Stephano, two Neapolitans scap'd!
Stephano	Prithee, do not turn me about. My stomach is not
	constant.
Caliban	(*aside*) These be fine things, an if they be not sprites.
	That's a brave god, and bears celestial liquor.
	I will kneel to him.
Stephano	How didst thou scape? How cam'st thou hither?
	Swear, by this bottle, how thou cam'st hither. I 120
	escap'd upon a butt of sack, which the sailors
	heaved o'erboard, by this bottle, which I made of
	the bark of a tree with mine own hands, since I
	was cast ashore.
Caliban	I'll swear upon that bottle, to be thy true subject,
	for the liquor is not earthly.
Stephano	Here. Swear, then, how thou escapedst. [127]
Trinculo	Swum ashore, man, like a duck. I can swim like a
	duck, I'll be sworn.
Stephano	Here, kiss the book. Though thou canst swim like 130
	a duck, thou art made like a goose.
Trinculo	O Stephano, hast any more of this?
Stephano	The whole butt, man. My cellar is in a rock by the
	sea-side, where my wine is hid. How now, moon-
	calf, how does thine ague?
Caliban	Hast thou not dropp'd from heaven?
Stephano	Out o' th' Moon, I do assure thee. I was the Man
	i' the Moon, when time was.
Caliban	I have seen thee in her, and I do adore thee. My
	mistress show'd me thee, and thy dog, and thy bush. 140

Stephano   Come, swear to that. Kiss the book. I will furnish
           It anon with new contents. Swear!
Trinculo   By this good light, this is a very shallow monster!
           I afeard of him? A very weak monster! The
           Man i' the Moon? A most poor credulous monster!
           Well drawn, monster, in good sooth!
Caliban   I'll show thee every fertile inch o' th' island, and
           I will kiss thy foot. I prithee be my god.
Trinculo   By this light, a most perfidious and drunken monster!
           When's god's asleep, he'll rob his bottle.   150
Caliban   I'll kiss thy foot. I'll swear myself thy subject.
Stephano   Come on then. Down, and swear!
Trinculo   I shall laugh myself to death at this puppy-headed
           monster. A most scurvy monster! I could find
           in my heart to beat him, –
Stephano   Come, kiss.
Trinculo   But that the poor monster's in drink. An abomin-
           able monster!
Caliban   I'll show thee the best springs, I'll pluck thee
               berries.
           I'll fish for thee, and get thee wood enough.   160
           A plague upon the tyrant that I serve!
           I'll bear him no more sticks, but follow thee,
           Thou wondrous man.
Trinculo   A most ridiculous monster, to make a wonder of a
           poor drunkard!
Caliban   I prithee let me bring thee where crabs grow;
           And I with my long nails will dig thee pig-nuts.
           Show thee a jay's nest, and instruct thee how
           To snare the nimble marmoset. I'll bring thee
           To clustering filberts, and sometimes I'll get thee   170
           Young scamels from the rock. Wilt thou go with
               me?
Stephano   I prithee now lead the way without any more talking.
           Trinculo, the King and all our company else being
           drown'd, we will inherit here. Here, bear my
           bottle. Fellow Trinculo, we'll fill him by and by
           again.

---

169.   **marmoset:** a small monkey
171.   **scamel:** unexplained, but perhaps a shellfish or a rock-nesting bird

Caliban	(*sings drunkenly*)
	Farewell, master! Farewell, farewell!
Trinculo	A howling monster! A drunken monster!
Caliban	No more dams I'll make for fish,
	Nor fetch in firing
	At requiring,
	Nor scrape trencher, nor wash dish.
	'Ban, 'Ban, Ca-caliban
	Has a new master. – Get a new man!
	Freedom, High-day! High-day, freedom! Freedom,
	hey-day, freedom!
Stephano	O brave monster! Lead the way.

180

Exeunt

INTERVAL

Act Third

Scene 1 [Scene 10]

Before Prospero's cell

Enter Ferdinand, bearing a log

Ferdinand There be some sports are painful, and their labour
Delight in them sets off. Some kinds of baseness
Are nobly undergone and most poor matters
Point to rich ends. This my mean task
Would be as heavy to me as odious, but
The mistress which I serve quickens what's dead,
And makes my labours pleasures. O, she is
Ten times more gentle than her father's crabbed,
And he's compos'd of harshness. I must remove
Some thousands of these logs, and pile them up,   10
Upon a sore injunction: my sweet mistress
Weeps when she sees me work, and says, such baseness
Had never like executor. I forget:
But these sweet thoughts do even refresh my labours,
Most busy lest when I do it.   [15]

Enter Miranda; and Prospero at a distance, unseen

Miranda   Alas, now, pray you,
Work not so hard. I would the lightning had
Burnt up those logs that you are enjoin'd to pile!
Pray set it down, and rest you. When this burns,

---

8. **crabbed:** ill-tempered   ◀**Ferdinand, Miranda, and Prospero**

57

	'Twill weep for having wearied you. My father
	Is hard at study. Pray now rest yourself, 20
	He's safe for these three hours.
Ferdinand	O most dear mistress,
	The sun will set before I shall discharge
	What I must strive to do.
Miranda	If you'll sit down,
	I'll bear your logs the while. Pray give me that,
	I'll carry it to the pile.
Ferdinand	No, precious creature,
	I had rather crack my sinews, break my back,
	Than you should such dishonour undergo,
	While I sit lazy by.
Miranda	It would become me
	As well as it does you, and I should do it
	With much more ease, for my good will is to it, 30
	And yours it is against.
Prospero	Poor worm, thou are infected!
	This visitation shows it.
Miranda	You look wearily.
Ferdinand	No, noble mistress, 'tis fresh morning with me
	When you are by at night. I do beseech you, –
	Chiefly that I might set it in my prayers, –
	What is your name?
Miranda	Miranda. – O my father,
	I have broke your hest to say so!
Ferdinand	Admir'd Miranda!
	Indeed the top of admiration, worth
	What's dearest to the world! Full many a lady
	I have ey'd with best regard, and many a time 40
	The harmony of their tongues hath into bondage
	Brought my too diligent ear. For several virtues
	Have I lik'd several women, never any
	With so full soul, but some defect in her
	Did quarrel with the noblest grace she ow'd,
	And put it to the foil. But you, O you,
	So perfect, and so peerless, are created
	Of every creature's best!
Miranda	I do not know

Ferdinand and Miranda

One of my sex; no woman's face remember,
Save, from my glass, mine own. For have I seen   50
More that I may call men than you, good friend,
And my dear father. How features are abroad
I am skilless of; but, by my modesty,
The jewel in my dower, I would not wish
Any companion in the world but you.
Nor can imagination form a shape,
Besides yourself, to like of. But I prattle
Something too wildly, and my father's precepts
I therein do forget.

Ferdinand   I am, in my condition,
A Prince, Miranda, I do think, a King,   60
I would not so, and would no more endure
This wooden slavery than to suffer
The flesh-fly blow my mouth. Hear my soul speak:
The very instant that I saw you, did
My heart fly to your service, there resides
To make me slave to it, and for your sake
Am I this patient log-man.

Miranda   Do you love me?
Ferdinand O heaven, O earth, bear witness to this sound,
And crown what I profess with kind event
If I speak true! If hollowly, invert   70
What best is boded me to mischief! I,
Beyond all limit of what else i' the world,
Do love, prize, honour you.

Miranda   I am a fool
To weep at what I am glad of.

Prospero   Fair encounter
Of two most rare affections! Heavens rain grace
On that which breeds between 'em!

Ferdinand   Wherefore weep you?
Miranda At mine unworthiness, that dare not offer
What I desire to give; and much less take
What I shall die to want. But this is trifling,
And all the more it seeks to hide itself,   80
The bigger bulk it shows. Hence, bashful cunning,
And prompt me, plain and holy innocence!
I am your wife, if you will marry me.

---

53. **skilless:** unknowledgeable

58. **precepts:** commands

	If not, I'll die your maid. To be your fellow
	You may deny me, but I'll be your servant
	Whether you will or no.
Ferdinand	My mistress, dearest,
	And I thus humble ever.
Miranda	My husband, then?
Ferdinand	Ay, with a heart as willing
	As bondage e'er of freedom! Here's my hand.
Miranda	And mine, with my heart in 't. And now farewell
	Till half an hour hence.
Ferdinand	A thousand thousand!

90

Exeunt Ferdinand and Miranda severally

Prospero	So glad of this as they I cannot be,
	Who are surpris'd withal, but my rejoicing
	At nothing can be more. I'll to my book,
	For yet ere supper-time must I perform
	Much business appertaining. *Exit*

Scene 2

Another part of the island

Enter Caliban, Stephano, and Trinculo

Stephano	Tell me not! – When the butt is out, we will drink water, not a drop before. Therefore bear up, and board 'em. Servant-monster, drink to me.
Trinculo	Servant-monster? The folly of this island! They say there's but five upon this isle. We are three of them. If th' other two be brain'd like us, the state totters.
Stephano	Drink, servant-monster, when I bid thee. Thy eyes are almost set in thy head.

Trinculo	Where should they be set else? He were a brave	10
	monster indeed, if they were set in his tail.	
Stephano	My man-monster hath drown'd his tongue in sack.	
	For my part, the sea cannot drown me, I swam, ere I	
	could recover the shore, five-and-thirty leagues off	
	and on, by this light, thou shalt be my lieutenant	
	monster, or my standard.	
Trinculo	Your lieutenant, if you list, he's no standard.	
Stephano	We'll not run, Monsieur Monster.	
Trinculo	Nor go neither, but you'll lie like dogs, and yet	
	say nothing neither.	20
Stephano	Moon-calf, speak once in thy life, if thou beest a	
	good moon-calf.	
Caliban	How does thy honour? Let me lick thy shoe. I'll	
	not serve him, he is not valiant.	
Trinculo	Thou liest, most ignorant monster! I am in case to	
	justle a constable. Why, thou debosh'd fish thou,	
	was there ever man a coward, that hath drunk so	
	much sack as I to-day? Wilt thou tell a monstrous	
	lie, being but half a fish and half a monster?	
Caliban	Lo, how he mocks me! Wilt thou let him, my lord?	30
Trinculo	'Lord,' quoth he? That a monster should be such	
	a natural!	
Caliban	Lo, lo, again! Bite him to death, I prithee.	
Stephano	Trinculo, keep a good tongue in your head. If you	
	prove a mutineer, the next tree! The poor mon-	
	ster's my subject, and he shall not suffer indignity.	
Caliban	I thank my noble lord. Wilt thou be pleas'd to	
	hearken once again to the suit I made to thee?	
Stephano	Marry, will I. Kneel, and repeat it. I will stand, and	
	so shall Trinculo.	40

Enter Ariel, invisible

Caliban	As I told thee before, I am subject to a tyrant, a
	sorcerer, that by his cunning hath cheated me of
	the island.
Ariel	Thou liest.

| 12. | **sack:** wine | 17. | **list/standard:** if he leans he will | 25. | **case:** fit state |
| 16. | **standard:** ensign | | not stand upright | 32. | **natural:** idiot |

Caliban	Thou liest, thou jesting monkey, thou.
	I would my valiant master would destroy thee!
	I do not lie.
Stephano	Trinculo, if you trouble him any more in's tale, by
	this hand, I will supplant some of your teeth.
Trinculo	Why, I said nothing. 50
Stephano	Mum then, and no more. Proceed.
Caliban	I say, by sorcery he got this isle.
	From me he got it. If thy greatness will
	Revenge it on him, for I know thou darest
	But this thing dare not.
Stephano	That's most certain.
Caliban	Thou shalt be lord of it, and I'll serve thee.
Stephano	How now shall this be compass'd? Canst thou
	bring me to the party?
Caliban	Yea, yea, my lord, I'll yield him thee asleep, 60
	Where thou mayst knock a nail into his head.
Ariel	Thou liest, thou canst not.
Caliban	What a pied ninny's this! Thou scurvy patch!
	I do beseech thy greatness give him blows,
	And take his bottle from him. When that's gone,
	He shall drink nought but brine, for I'll not show him
	Where the quick freshes are.
Stephano	Trinculo, run into no further danger. Interrupt the
	monster one word further, and, by this hand, I'll
	turn my mercy out o' doors, and make a stock-fish 70
	of thee.
Trinculo	Why, what did I? I did nothing. I'll go farther
	off.
Stephano	Didst thou not say he lied?
Ariel	Thou liest.
Stephano	Did I so? Take thou that. (*Beats him.*) As you like
	this, give me the lie another time.
Trinculo	I did not give the lie. Out o' your wits, and hear-
	ing too? A pox o' your bottle! This can sack and
	drinking do. A murrain on your monster, and the 80
	devil take your fingers!
Caliban	Ha, ha, ha!

58.	**compass'd:** accomplished	70.	**stock-fish:** pounded saltfish
63.	**patch:** clown	80.	**murrain:** cattle disease

Nicholas Pennell as
Stephano with Caliban

Stephano	Now, forward with your tale. – Prithee, stand farther off.
Caliban	Beat him enough. After a little time, I'll beat him too.
Stephano	Stand farther. Come, proceed.
Caliban	Why, as I told thee, 'tis a custom with him I' th' afternoon to sleep. There thou mayst brain him. Having first seiz'd his books; or with a log Batter his skull, or paunch him with a stake, Or cut his wezand with thy knife. Remember First to possess his books, for without them He's but a sot, as I am, nor hath not One spirit to command. They all do hate him As rootedly as I. Burn but his books. He has brave utensils, for so he calls them, Which, when he has a house, he'll deck withal. And that most deeply to consider is The beauty of his daughter. He himself Calls her a nonpareil. I never saw a woman, But only Sycorax my dam, and she, But she as far surpasseth Sycorax As great'st does least.
Stephano	Is it so brave a lass?
Caliban	Ay, lord, she will become thy bed, I warrant, And bring thee forth brave brood.
Stephano	Monster, I will kill this man. His daughter and I will be King and Queen, – save our graces! – and Trinculo and thyself shall be viceroys. Dost thou like the plot, Trinculo?
Trinculo	Excellent.
Stephano	Give me thy hand, I am sorry I beat thee; but, while thou liv'st, keep a good tongue in thy head.
Caliban	Within this half hour will he be asleep. Wilt thou destroy him then?
Stephano	Ay, on mine honour.
Ariel	This will I tell my master.

90

100

110

---

90. **paunch him:** stab him in the belly   91. **wezand:** windpipe   96. **utensils:** furnishings

93. **sot:** fool   100. **nonpareil:** without equal

Caliban   Thou mak'st me merry. I am full of pleasure,
          Let us be jocund! Will you troll the catch
          You taught me but while-ere?
Stephano At thy request, monster, I will do reason, any reason.
          – Come on, Trinculo, let us sing.   *Sings:*   120
                  Flout 'em and scout 'em,
                  And scout 'em and flout 'em;
                      Thought is free.
Caliban   That's not the tune.

Ariel plays the tune on a tabor and pipe

Stephano What is this same?
Trinculo This is the tune of our catch, play'd by the picture
          of Nobody.
Stephano If thou beest a man, show thyself in thy likeness.
          If thou beest a devil, tak't as thou list.
Trinculo O, forgive me my sins!   130
Stephano He that dies pays all debts. I defy thee. Mercy
          upon us!
Caliban   Art thou afeard?
Stephano No, monster, not I.
Caliban   Be not afeard, the isle is full of noises,
          Sounds, and sweet airs, that give delight, and hurt not.
          Sometimes a thousand twangling instruments
          Will hum about mine ears; and sometimes voices,
          That, if I then had wak'd after long sleep,
          Will make me sleep again, and then, in dreaming,   140
          The clouds methought would open, and show riches
          Ready to drop upon me, that when I wak'd,
          I cried to dream again.
Stephano This will prove a brave kingdom to me, where
          I shall have my music for nothing.
Caliban   When Prospero is destroy'd.
Stephano That shall be by and by. I remember the story.
Trinculo The sound is going away, let's follow it, and after
          do our work.
Stephano Lead, monster, we'll follow. I would I could see   150
          this taborer! He lays it on.
Trinculo Wilt come? I'll follow, Stephano.   *Exeunt*

117. **troll the catch:** sing the song
151. **taborer:** drummer

Scene 3

Another part of the island

Enter Alonso, Sebastian, Antonio, Gonzalo, Adrian, Francisco, and others

Gonzalo	By 'r lakin, I can go no further, sir,
	My old bones ache. Here's a maze trod indeed
	Through forth-rights and meanders! By your patience,
	I needs must rest me.
Alonso	Old lord, I cannot blame thee,
	Who am myself attach'd with weariness
	To the dulling of my spirits. Sit down, and rest.
	Even here I will put off my hope, and keep it
	No longer for my flatterer. He is drown'd
	Whom thus we stray to find, and the sea mocks
	Our frustrate search on land. Well, let him go.

Alonso's line 10 is marked with the number 10 in the margin.

Antonio (*aside to Sebastian*) I am right glad that he's so out of hope.
Do not for one repulse forego the purpose
That you resolv'd to 'ffect.
Sebastian   (*aside to Antonio*) The next advantage
Will we take thoroughly.
Antonio   (*aside to Sebastian*) Let it be to-night,
For, now they are oppress'd with travel, they
Will not, nor cannot use such vigilance
As when they are fresh.
Sebastian   (*aside to Antonio*) I say to-night. No more.

Solemn and strange music

Alonso What harmony is this? – My good friends, hark!
Gonzalo Marvellous sweet music!

*Enter Prospero above, invisible. Enter several strange Shapes,
bringing in a banquet: they dance about it with gentle actions
of salutations; and, inviting the King, etc. to eat, they depart*

Alonso Give us kind keepers, heavens! – What were these?   20
Sebastian A living drollery. Now I will believe
That there are unicorns; that in Arabia

---

1. **By'r lakin:** by your Lady Kind (Virgin Mary)
3. **forth-rights and meanders:** paths sometimes straight, sometimes twisted
21. **living drollery:** puppet show with live players

There is one tree, the phoenix' throne, one phoenix
At this hour reigning there.
Antonio   I'll believe both;
And what does else want credit, come to me,
And I'll be sworn 'tis true. Travellers ne'er did lie,
Though fools at home condemn 'em.
Gonzalo   If in Naples
I should report this now, would they believe me?
If I should say, I saw such islanders,
For certes, these are people of the island,   30
Who, though they are of monstrous shape, yet note,
Their manners are more gentle-kind than of
Our human generation you shall find
Many, nay, almost any.
Prospero   (*aside*) Honest lord,
Thou hast said well, for some of you there present
Are worse than devils.
Alonso   I cannot too much muse
Such shapes, such gesture, and such sound, expressing,
Although they want the use of tongue, a kind
Of excellent dumb discourse.
Prospero   (*aside*) Praise in departing.
Francisco They vanish'd strangely.
Sebastian   No matter, since   40
They have left their viands behind, for we have
     stomachs.
Will't please you taste of what is here?
Alonso   Not I.
Gonzalo Faith, sir, you need not fear. When we were boys,
Who would believe that there were mountaineers
Dew-lapped like bulls, whose throats had hanging
     at 'em
Wallets of flesh? Or that there were such men
Whose heads stood in their breasts which now
     we find.
Each putter-out of five for one will bring us
Good warrant of.
Alonso   I will stand to, and feed,
Although my last, no matter, since I feel   50
The best is past. Brother, my lord the Duke,
Stand to, and do as we.

---

30. **certes:** assuredly   45. **dew-lap:** loose skin that hangs from the neck of cattle
36. **muse:** wonder at   48. **putter-out:** a traveller depositing a sum was repaid
41. **viands:** provisions   fivefold if he could prove he had gone to his destination.

THE TEMPEST

GONZALO AND
ADRIAN.

HEELEY '82

Thunder and lightning. Enter Ariel, like a harpy; claps his wings upon the table; and, with a quaint device, the banquet vanishes

Ariel   You are three men of sin, whom Destiny,
That hath to instrument this lower world,
And what is in't, the never-surfeited sea
Hath caus'd to belch up you, and on this island,
Where man doth not inhabit, you 'mongst men
Being most unfit to live. I have made you mad;
And even with such-like valour men hang and drown
Their proper selves.

Alonso, Sebastian, etc. draw their swords

              You fools! I and my fellows   60
Are ministers of Fate, the elements,
Of whom your swords are temper'd, may as well
Wound the loud winds, or with bemock'd-at stabs
Kill the still-closing waters, as diminish
One dowle that's in my plume. My fellow-ministers
Are like invulnerable. If you could hurt,
Your swords are now too massy for your strengths,
And will not be uplifted. But remember,
For that's my business to you, that you three
From Milan did supplant good Prospero,   70
Expos'd unto the sea, which hath requit it,
Him and his innocent child: for which foul deed,
The powers, delaying, not forgetting, have
Incens'd the seas and the shores, yea, all the creatures,
Against your peace. Thee of thy son, Alonso,
They have bereft; and do pronounce by me
Lingering perdition, worse than any death
Can be at once, shall step by step attend
You and your ways, whose wraths to guard you from,
Which here, in this most desolate isle, else falls   80
Upon your heads, is nothing but heart's-sorrow,
And a clear life ensuing.

He vanishes in thunder; then, to soft music, enter the Shapes again, and dance, with mocks and mows, and carrying out the table.

(stage direction) **harpy:** a fabulous winged monster, supposed to act as a minister of divine vengeance	65.	**dowle:** featherdown
	67.	**massy:** massive
	71.	**requit:** avenged

Prospero	Bravely the figure of this harpy hast thou

Prospero Bravely the figure of this harpy hast thou
Perform'd, my Ariel. A grace it had, devouring.
Of my instruction hast thou nothing bated
In what thou hadst to say. So, with good life
And observation strange, my meaner ministers
Their several kinds have done. My high charms work,
And these mine enemies are all knit up
In their distractions. They now are in my power,　　90
And in these fits I leave them, while I visit
Young Ferdinand, whom they suppose is drown'd,
And his and mine lov'd darling.　　　　*Exit above*

Gonzalo I' the name of something holy, sir, why stand you
In this strange stare?

Alonso　　　　　　　O, it is monstrous! Monstrous!
Methought the billows spoke, and told me of it,
The winds did sing it to me, and the thunder,
That deep and dreadful organ-pipe, pronounc'd
The name of Prosper. It did bass my trespass,
Therefore my son i' th' ooze is bedded, and　　100
I'll seek him deeper than e'er plummet sounded,
And with him there lie mudded.　　　　*Exit*

Sebastian　　　　　　　But one fiend at a time,
I'll fight their legions o'er.

Antonio　　　　　　　I'll be thy second.

Exeunt Sebastian and Antonio

Gonzalo All three of them are desperate. Their great guilt
Like poison given to work a greater time after,
Now 'gins to bite the spirits. I do beseech you
That are of suppler joints follow them swiftly,　　[107]
And hinder them from what this ecstasy　　[108]
May now provoke them to.

Adrian　　　　　　　Follow, I pray you.　　*Exeunt*　[109]

99.　**bass:** proclaim in deep bass tones
108.　**ecstasy:** madness

Scene 1

[Scene 13]

Before Prospero's cell

Enter Prospero, Ferdinand, and Miranda

Prospero If I have too austerely punish'd you,
Your compensation makes amends, for I
Have given you here a third of mine own life,
Or that for which I live; who once again
I tender to thy hand. All thy vexations
Were but my trials of thy love, and thou
Hast strangely stood the test. Here, afore Heaven,
I ratify this my rich gift. O Ferdinand,
Do not smile at me, that I boast her off,
For thou shalt find she will outstrip all praise,   10
And make it halt behind her.

Ferdinand   I do believe it
Against an oracle.

Prospero Then, as my gift, and thine own acquisition
Worthily purchas'd, take my daughter, but
If thou dost break her virgin-knot before
All sanctimonious ceremonies may
With full and holy rite be minister'd,
No sweet aspersion shall the heavens let fall
To make this contract grow, but barren hate,
Sour-eyed disdain and discord shall bestrew   20
The union of your bed with weeds so loathly

---

7. **strangely:** rarely

18. **sweet aspersion:** blessing

◀ **Ariel as a harpy**

73

That you shall hate it both. Therefore take heed,
As Hymen's lamps shall light you.

Ferdinand   As I hope
For quiet days, fair issue and long life,
With such love as 'tis now, the murkiest den,
The most opportune place, the strong'st suggestion
Our worser genius can, shall never melt
Mine honour into lust, to take away
The edge of that day's celebration,
When I shall think, or Phoebus' steeds are founder'd,   30
Or Night keep chain'd below.

Prospero   Fairly spoke.
Sit, then, and talk with her, she is thine own.
What, Ariel! My industrious servant, Ariel!

Enter Ariel

Ariel   What would my potent master? Here I am.
Prospero Thou and thy meaner fellows your last service
Did worthily perform, and I must use you
In such another trick. Go bring the rabble
O'er whom I give thee power, here to this place:
Incite them to quick motion, for I must
Bestow upon the eyes of this young couple   40
Some vanity of mine art. It is my promise,
And they expect it from me.

Ariel   Presently?
Prospero Ay, with a twink.
Ariel   Before you can say, 'come,' and 'go,'
And breathe twice, and cry, 'so, so,'
Each one, tripping on his toe,
Will be here with mop and mow.
Do you love me, master? No?
Prospero Dearly, my delicate Ariel. Do not approach
Till thou dost hear me call.
Ariel   Well, I conceive.   *Exit*   50
Prospero Look thou be true. Do not give dalliance
Too much the rein. The strongest oaths are straw
To the fire i' the blood. Be more abstemious,
Or else, good night your vow!

---

23. **Hymen:** Roman God of marriage	35. **meaner:** inferior
27. **worser genius:** bad angel	41. **vanity:** show
30. **Phoebus:** Apollo, the Sun God	51. **dalliance:** amorous toying

Ferdinand   I warrant you, sir,
The white cold virgin snow upon my heart
Abates the ardour of my liver.
Prospero   Well.
Now come, my Ariel! Bring a corollary,
Rather than want a spirit. Appear, and pertly!
No tongue! All eyes! Be silent.   *Soft music*

Enter Iris   [Scene 14]

Iris   Ceres, most bounteous lady, thy rich leas   [60-138]
Of wheat, rye, barley, vetches, oats, and pease;
Thy turfy mountains, where live nibbling sheep,
And flat meads thatch'd with stover, them to keep;
Thy banks with pioned and twilled brims,
Which spongy April at thy hest betrims,
To make cold nymphs chaste crowns; and thy
    broom-groves,
Whose shadow the dismissed bachelor loves,
Being lass-lorn; thy pole-clipt vineyard;
And thy sea-marge, sterile and rocky-hard,
Where thou thyself dost air; – the Queen o' the sky,   70
Whose watery arch and messenger am I,
Bids thee leave these, and with her sovereign grace,
Here, on this grass-plot, in this very place,
To come and sport: – her peacocks fly amain:

Juno appears in her car above

Approach, rich Ceres, her to entertain.

Enter Ceres

Ceres   Hail, many-colour'd messenger, that ne'er
Dost disobey the wife of Jupiter;
Who, with thy saffron wings, upon my flowers
Diffusest honey-drops, refreshing showers,
And with each end of thy blue bow dost crown   80
My bosky acres and my unshrubb'd down,
Rich scarf to my proud earth; – why hath thy Queen

	Summon'd me hither, to this short-grass'd green?
Iris	A contract of true love to celebrate,
	And some donation freely to estate
	On the bless'd lovers.

Ceres   Tell me, heavenly bow,
If Venus or her son, as thou dost know,
Do now attend the Queen? Since they did plot
The means that dusky Dis my daughter got,
Her, and her blind boy's scandal'd company,   90
I have forsworn.

Iris   Of her society
Be not afraid: I met her deity
Cutting the clouds towards Paphos; and her son
Dove-drawn with her: here thought they to have done
Some wanton charm upon this man and maid,
Whose vows are, that no bed-right shall be paid
Till Hymen's torch be lighted: but in vain;
Mars's hot minion is return'd again,
Her waspish-headed son has broke his arrows,
Swears he will shoot no more, but play with sparrows,   100
And be a boy right out.

Ceres   High'st Queen of state,
Great Juno, comes; I know her by her gait.

Enter Juno

Juno   How does my bounteous sister? Go with me
To bless this twain, that they may prosperous be,
And honour'd in their issue.   *They sing:*

Juno   Honour, riches, marriage-blessing,
Long continuance, and increasing,
Hourly joys be still upon you!
Juno sings her blessings on you.

Ceres   Earth's increase, foison plenty,   110
Barns and garners never empty;
Vines with clustering bunches growing;
Plants with goodly burthen bowing;
Spring come to you at the farthest
In the very end of harvest!
Scarcity and want shall shun you;

	Ceres' blessing so is on you.	
Ferdinand	This is a most majestic vision, and	
	Harmonious charmingly. May I be bold	
	To think these spirits?	
Prospero	Spirits, which by mine art	120
	I have from their confines call'd to enact	
	My present fancies.	
Ferdinand	Let me live here ever;	
	So rare a wonder'd father and a wise	
	Makes this place Paradise.	

Juno and Ceres whisper, and send Iris on employment

Prospero	Sweet, now, silence!	
	Juno and Ceres whisper seriously;	
	There's something else to do: hush, and be mute,	
	Or else our spell is marr'd.	
Iris	You nymphs call'd Naiads of the windring brooks,	
	With your sedg'd crowns, and ever-harmless looks,	
	Leave your crisp channels, and on this green land	130
	Answer your summons; Juno does command:	
	Come, temperate nymphs, and help to celebrate	
	A contract of true love; be not too late.	

Enter certain Nymphs

You sunburn'd sicklemen, of August weary,
Come hither from the furrow, and be merry,
Make holiday; your rye-straw hats put on,
And these fresh nymphs encounter every one
In country footing.

*Enter certain Reapers, properly habited: they join with the
Nymphs in a graceful dance; towards the end whereof
Prospero starts suddenly, and speaks; after which, to a
strange, hollow, and confused noise, they heavily vanish.*

Prospero	(*aside*) I had forgot that foul conspiracy	[Scene 15]
	Of the beast Caliban and his confederates	140
	Against my life. The minute of their plot	

1.

3.

4. CERES - 2 STEPS SL
IRIS x UR x US of FERDINAND (h S-)
5. McKAN FOLLOWS to SL on 2ND
FERDINAND + MIRANDA x DC
KELLY x SR of CERES

7. KELLER + ROCH ENTER BALCON/K-SR/R-SL
CERES x UL
8. KELLY FOLLOW to 2ND SL STEP /FERDINAND+MIRANDA x DL on 2ND
IRIS x DR on 3RD
McKAN FOLLOWS to DR in CENTER

10. JUNO TRUCK JUST/.. BALCONY / PROSPERO x DC on 3RD
11. IR.S x DR on DECK/CER.. x UL on CS / IRIS x SR on CS / CERES x SL on CS
12. IR.S x CERES (S) AC CS. CERES x UR. IR... BOYS/CERES BOY/IRIS+CERES BOY
13. ARIEL - BOYS ENTER UL w/BENCHES
14. ARIEL x DL /LEADS FERDINAND+MIRANDA to CS
DOUBLE LEADS to SR on ...
15. COL/OS LEADS to DL on ...
ARIEL x SL on 3RD

ZEDDIK, GIBSON/BINSLEY, CLARK, SPREAD to CS
17. DORELL, SIMPSON/ARIEL, COL/COS SPREAD US

18. BOYS x onto 2ND
19. BOYS x onto 1ST
20. BOYS x onto DECK
21. BOYS KNEEL
22. BOYS BRING ... in to FERDINAND+MIRANDA
23. ARIEL LEADS ... 1x... FERDINAND+MIRANDA
24. BOYS x onto 3RD (B) POSITIONS) / ARIEL x C-PILLAR

LITES 116.1 - SL?
EM LITES 117 (DOWN)
A.F. 117 -STAIR P.

LITES 118 - JUNO (1...)

LITES 119 CIRCLE+...

LITES 11B.S /71...
RESTORE D...

LITES 120 - P.DC 1 (3...

BOYS ENTRANCE

1. COLIC
2. DORELL
3. CLARK
4. SIMP...
5. BINSLEY
6. GIBSON
7. ZEDDIK

25. MASS xit:	UC	R.TUNNEL	L.TUNNEL	R.LOUVRE	L.LOUVRE	BALC
	EVANS	DORELL	BINSLEY	KRELLER	ROCH	JUNO
	HAZEL	SIMPSON	CLARK			
	McKAN	GIBSON	COLICOS			
	KELLY	ZEDDIK				
	CERES					
	IRIS					
	WALKIN					
	ROCH					

Pages from the stage manager's prompt book
showing the blocking for the Masque sequence

78

CERES: Hail, many-coloured messenger,
Who, with saffron wings, upon my flowers
Diffusest honey-drops, refreshing showers;
4 Why hath thy queen summoned me hither
To this short grassed green?

IRIS: 5 A contract of true love to celebrate,
And some donation freely to bestow
On the blessed lovers.

CERES: 8 Great Juno comes; I know her by her gait.

JUNO: Come with me
To bless this twain, that they may prosperous be,
And honoured in their issue.
You sunburned sicklemen, of August weary,
Come hither from the furrow, and be merry.
Be merry, be merry, be merry, be merry,
12 Make holiday, make holiday, make holiday.

13 CHORUS: Honour, riches, marriage blessing,
Long continuance, and increasing,
15 Hourly joys be still upon you!
Juno sings her blessings on you.

Earth's increase, foison plenty,
Barns and garners never empty,
17 Vines with clustering bunches growing,
Plants with goodly burden bowing;
18 Spring come to you at the farthest
19 In the very end of harvest.
20 Scarcity and want shall shun you,
21 Ceres' blessing so is on you.

22 Earth's increase, foison plenty,
Barns and garners never empty,
23 Vines with clustering bunches growing,
Plants with goodly burden bowing.
Spring come to you at the farthest
In the very end of harvest.
Scarcity and want shall shun you,
24 Ceres' blessing so is on you.

Handwritten annotations (lighting and sound cues):

WAR. BALCONY / R. LOUVRE / L. LOUVRE / SOUND
LITES 116.1
C. LITE R. LOUVRE / L. LOUVRE
2ND WARNING ON SMOKE // LITES 117 + TRUCK...
LITES 118
Q-LITE BALCONY (FAN) SOUND (MUS.CUE)
LITES 118
WAR. LIC / R. TUNNEL / L. TUNNEL
LITES 118.5
Q-LITE R. TUNNEL / L. TUNNEL
SMOKE OUT
Q-LITE LIC / LITES 119
LITES 119.5
WARN. RUCK +?
LITES 119.6
WAR. R. DOOR / L. DOOR / L. TUNNEL
LITES 119.7
LITES 120 + 120.1...   "GO" L. TUNNEL "GO"   TRACK OFF

	Is almost come. (*to the Spirits*) Well done! Avoid!
	No more!
Ferdinand	This is strange. Your father's in some passion
	That works him strongly.
Miranda	Never till this day
	Saw I him touch'd with anger, so distemper'd.
Prospero	You do look, my son, in a moved sort,

As if you were dismay'd. Be cheerful, sir.
Our revels now are ended. These our actors,
As I foretold you, were all spirits, and
Are melted into air, into thin air,   150
And like the baseless fabric of this vision,
The cloud-capp'd towers, the gorgeous palaces,
The solemn temples, the great globe itself,
Yea, all which it inherit, shall dissolve,
And like this insubstantial pageant faded,
Leave not a rack behind. We are such stuff
As dreams are made on; and our little life
Is rounded with a sleep. Sir, I am vex'd.
Bear with my weakness, my old brain is troubled.
Be not disturb'd with my infirmity.   160
If you be pleas'd, retire into my cell,
And there repose, a turn or two I'll walk,
To still my beating mind.

Ferdinand	
Miranda	We wish your peace. *Exeunt*
Prospero	Come with a thought. I thank thee, Ariel. Come.

Enter Ariel [Scene 16]

Ariel	Thy thoughts I cleave to, what's thy pleasure?
Prospero	Spirit,
	We must prepare to meet with Caliban.
Ariel	Ay, my commander, when I presented Ceres,
	I thought to have told thee of it, but I fear'd
	Lest I might anger thee.
Prospero	Say again, where didst thou leave these varlets? 170
Ariel	I told you, sir, they were red-hot with drinking,
	So full of valour, that they smote the air

| 151. | **baseless:** insubstantial | 165: | **cleave:** adhere |
| 156. | **rack:** cloud | 170. | **varlets:** ruffians |

For breathing in their faces, beat the ground
For kissing of their feet, yet always bending
Towards their project. Then I beat my tabor,
At which, like unback'd colts they prick'd their ears,
Advanc'd their eyelids, lifted up their noses
As they smelt music. So I charm'd their ears,
That, calf-like, they my lowing follow'd, through
Tooth'd briers, sharp furzes, pricking goss, and
    thorns,   180
Which enter'd their frail shins. At last I left them
I' th' filthy-mantled pool beyond your cell,
There dancing up to the chins, that the foul lake
O'erstunk their feet.

Prospero   This was well done, my bird.
Thy shape invisible retain thou still:
The trumpery in my house, go bring it hither,
For stale to catch these thieves.

Ariel   I go, I go.   *Exit*

Prospero A devil, a born devil, on whose nature
Nurture can never stick. On whom my pains,
Humanely taken, all, all lost, quite lost,   190
And as with age his body uglier grows,
So his mind cankers. I will plague them all,
Even to roaring.

Re-enter Ariel, loaden with glistering apparel, etc.   [Scene 17]

Come, hang them on this line.

Prospero and Ariel remain, invisible

Enter Caliban, Stephano, and Trinculo, all wet

Caliban   Pray you, tread softly, that the blind mole may not
Hear a foot fall. We now are near his cell.

Stephano Monster, your fairy, which you say is a harmless fairy,
has done little better than play'd the Jack with us.

Trinculo Monster, I do smell all horse-piss, at which my nose
is in great indignation.   200

Stephano So is mine. Do you hear, monster? If I should

172.	**smote:** hit at	182. **filthy-mantled:** scum-covered	194. **line:** lime tree
176.	**unback'd:** unbroken	187. **stale:** decoy	198. **Jack:** knave

Pages from the score composed by
Stanley Silverman for "The Tempest"

Caliban, Stephano, and Trinculo, played by John Jarvis

	take a displeasure against you, look you, –	
Trinculo	Thou wert but a lost monster.	
Caliban	Good my lord, give me thy favour still.	
	Be patient, for the prize I'll bring thee to	
	Shall hoodwink this mischance. Therefore speak softly,	
	All's hush'd as midnight yet.	
Trinculo	Ay, but to lose our bottles in the pool, –	
Stephano	There is not only disgrace and dishonour in that,	
	monster, but an infinite loss.	210
Trinculo	That's more to me than my wetting. Yet this is	
	your harmless fairy, monster.	
Stephano	I will fetch off my bottle, though I be o'er ears for	
	my labour.	
Caliban	Prithee, my king, be quiet, See'st thou here,	
	This is the mouth o' the cell. No noise, and enter.	
	Do that good mischief, which may make this island	
	Thine own for ever, and I, thy Caliban,	
	For aye thy foot-licker.	
Stephano	Give me thy hand. I do begin to have bloody	220
	thoughts.	
Trinculo	O King Stephano! O peer! O worthy Stephano!	
	Look what a wardrobe here is for thee!	
Caliban	Let it alone, thou fool, it is but trash.	
Trinculo	O, ho, monster! We know what belongs to a frippery.	
	O King Stephano!	[226]
Stephano	Put off that gown, Trinculo, by this hand I'll have	
	that gown.	
Trinculo	Thy grace shall have it.	
Caliban	The dropsy drown this fool! What do you mean	230
	To dote thus on such luggage? Let's alone,	
	And do the murder first. If he awake,	
	From toe to crown he'll fill our skins with pinches,	
	Make us strange stuff.	
Stephano	Be you quiet, monster. Mistress line, is not this	
	my jerkin? Now is the jerkin under the line. Now,	[236-38]
	jerkin, you are like to lose your hair, and prove a bald	
	jerkin.	
Trinculo	Do, do! We steal by line and level, an't like your	[239-40]
	grace.	240
Stephano	I thank thee for that jest. Here's a garment for 't.	

206.	**hoodwink:** render this misfortune harmless	236.	**jerkin:** jacket
	and put it out of sight	239.	**by line and level:** by the rules
230.	**dropsy:** fluid in the body's connective tissue		

	Wit shall not go unrewarded while I am King of this	
	country. 'Steal by line and level' is an excellent	[243-44]
	pass of pate. There's another garment for 't.	
Trinculo	Monster, come, put some lime upon your fingers,	
	and away with the rest.	
Caliban	I will have none on 't. We shall lose our time,	
	And all be turn'd to barnacles, or to apes	
	With foreheads villanous low.	
Stephano	Monster, lay-to your fingers. Help to bear this away	250
	where my hogshead of wine is, or I'll turn you out	
	of my kingdom. Go to, carry this.	
Trinculo	And this.	
Stephano	Ay, and this.	

A noise of hunters heard. Enter divers Spirits, in shape of
dogs and hounds, hunting them about; Prospero and
Ariel setting them on

Prospero	Hey, Mountain, hey!	[Scene 17A]
Ariel	Silver! There it goes, Silver!	
Prospero	Fury, Fury! There, Tyrant, there! Hark, hark!	

Caliban, Stephano, and Trinculo are driven out

	Go, charge my goblins that they grind their joints	
	With dry convulsions, shorten up their sinews	
	With aged cramps, and more pinch-spotted make them	260
	Than pard or cat o' mountain.	
Ariel	Hark, they roar!	
Prospero	Let them be hunted soundly. At this hour	
	Lies at my mercy all mine enemies.	
	Shortly shall all my labours end, and thou	
	Shalt have the air at freedom. For a little	
	Follow, and do me service.	*Exeunt*

---

245. **lime:** bird lime, which is a sticky substance
248. **barnacles:** geese
260. **pard or cat o' mountain:** leopard or cougar

Act Fifth

Scene 1

Before the cell of Prospero

Enter Prospero, in his magic robes, and Ariel

Prospero Now does my project gather to a head.
My charms crack not. My spirits obey, and time
Goes upright with his carriage. How's the day?
Ariel On the sixth hour, at which time, my lord,
You said our work should cease.
Prospero   I did say so,
When first I rais'd the tempest. Say, my spirit,
How fares the King and 's followers?
Ariel   Confin'd together
In the same fashion as you gave in charge,
Just as you left them, all prisoners, sir,
In the line-grove which weather-fends your cell.   10
They cannot budge till your release. The King,
His brother, and yours, abide all three distracted,
And the remainder mourning over them,
Brimful of sorrow and dismay; but chiefly
Him that you term'd sir, 'The good old lord,
   Gonzalo',
His tears runs down his beard, like winter's drops
From eaves of reeds. Your charm so strongly
   works 'em,
That if you now beheld them, your affections

---

10. **line-grove:** limegrove
      weather-fends: protects from the weather
17. **eaves of reeds:** thatched roofs

	Would become tender.	
Prospero	Dost thou think so, spirit?	
Ariel	Mine would, sir, were I human.	
Prospero	And mine shall.	20

Has thou, which art but air, a touch, a feeling
Of their afflictions, and shall not myself,
One of their kind, that relish all as sharply,
Passion as they, be kindlier mov'd than thou art?
Though with their high wrongs I am struck to the
   quick,
Yet with my nobler reason 'gainst my fury
Do I take part. The rarer action is
In virtue than in vengeance. They being penitent,
The sole drift of my purpose doth extend
Not a frown further. Go, release them, Ariel,   30
My charms I'll break, their senses I'll restore,
And they shall be themselves.

Ariel   I'll fetch them, sir.   *Exit*

Prospero Ye elves of hills, brooks, standing lakes, and groves,
And ye, that on the sands with printless foot
Do chase the ebbing Neptune, and do fly him
When he comes back; you demi-puppets, that
By moonshine do the green sour ringlets make,
Whereof the ewe not bites; and you, whose pastime
Is to make midnight mushrooms, that rejoice
To hear the solemn curfew, by whose aid   40
Weak masters though ye be, I have bedimm'd
The noontide sun, call'd forth the mutinous winds,
And 'twixt the green sea, and the azur'd vault
Set roaring war. To the dread rattling thunder
Have I given fire, and rifted Jove's stout oak
With his own bolt; the strong-bas'd promontory
Have I made shake, and by the spurs pluck'd up
The pine and cedar. Graves at my command
Have wak'd their sleepers, op'd, and let 'em forth
By my so potent art. But this rough magic   50
I here abjure, and, when I have requir'd
Some heavenly music, which even now I do,
To work mine end upon their senses that

---

24. **passion:** feel
36. **demi-puppets:** small fairies
37. **green sour ringlets:** fairy rings in the grass

This airy charm is for, I'll break my staff,
Bury it certain fathoms in the earth,
And deeper than did ever plummet sound
I'll drown my book.   *Solemn music*

Re-enter Ariel before: then Alonso, with a frantic   [Scene 19]
gesture, attended by Gonzalo; Sebastian and Antonio
in like manner attended by Adrian and Francisco: they
all enter the circle which Prospero had made, and there
stand charmed; which Prospero observing, speaks:

A solemn air, and the best comforter
To an unsettled fancy, cure thy brains
Now useless, boil within thy skull! There stand,   60
For you are spell-stopp'd.
Holy Gonzalo, honourable man,
Mine eyes, ev'n sociable to the show of thine,
Fall fellowly drops. The charm dissolves apace,
And as the morning steals upon the night,
Melting the darkness, so their rising senses
Begin to chase the ignorant fumes that mantle
Their clearer reason. O good Gonzalo,
My true preserver, and a loyal sir
To him thou follow'st! I will pay thy graces   70
Home both in word and deed. Most cruelly
Didst thou, Alonso, use me and my daughter.
Thy brother was a furtherer in the act.
Thou art pinch'd for't now, Sebastian. Flesh and
     blood,
You, brother mine, that entertain'd ambition,
Expell'd remorse and nature, who, with Sebastian,
Whose inward pinches therefore are most strong,
Would here have kill'd your King, I do forgive thee,
Unnatural though thou art. Their understanding
Begins to swell, and the approaching tide   80
Will shortly fill the reasonable shore,
That now lies foul and muddy. Not one of them
That yet looks on me, or would know me. Ariel,
Fetch me the hat and rapier in my cell.   [84]

63.   **sociable:** sympathetic.
67.   **mantle:** conceal

Alonso and Prospero

I will discase me, and myself present
As I was sometime Milan. Quickly, spirit,
Thou shalt ere long be free.

Ariel sings and helps to attire him

        Where the bee sucks, there suck I,
        In a cowslip's bell I lie,
        There I couch when owls do cry.   90
        On the bat's back I do fly
        After summer merrily.
        Merrily, merrily shall I live now
        Under the blossom that hangs on the bough.

Prospero   Why, that's my dainty Ariel! I shall miss thee,
But yet thou shalt have freedom. So, so, so.
To the King's ship, invisible as thou art,
There shalt thou find the mariners asleep
Under the hatches. The Master and the Boatswain
Being awake, enforce them to this place,   100
And presently, I prithee.

Ariel   I drink the air before me, and return
Or ere your pulse twice beat.   *Exit*

Gonzalo   All torment, trouble, wonder and amazement   [Scene 20]
Inhabits here. Some heavenly power guide us
Out of this fearful country!

Prospero   Behold, sir King,
The wronged Duke of Milan, Prospero.
For more assurance that a living Prince
Does now speak to thee, I embrace thy body,
And to thee and thy company I bid   110
A hearty welcome.

Alonso   Whe'er thou be'st he or no,
Or some enchanted trifle to abuse me,
As late I have been, I not know. Thy pulse
Beats, as of flesh and blood; and, since I saw thee,
The affliction of my mind amends, with which,
I fear'd, a madness held me. This must crave –
An if this be at all – a most strange story.
Thy dukedom I resign, and do entreat
Thou pardon me my wrongs. – But how should
    Prospero

---

111. **whe'er:** whether
116. **crave:** require

Gonzalo, Adrian, Prospero,
Alonso, Ferdinand, and Miranda

	Be living, and be here?	
Prospero	First, noble friend,	120
	Let me embrace thine age, whose honour cannot	
	Be measur'd or confin'd.	
Gonzalo	Whether this be	
	Or be not, I'll not swear.	
Prospero	You do yet taste	

Some subtleties o' the isle, that will not let you
Believe things certain. Welcome, my friends all!
(*aside to Sebastian and Antonio*) But you, my brace of lords,
    were I so minded,
I here could pluck his highness' frown upon you,
And justify you traitors. At this time
I will tell no tales.

Sebastian   (*aside*) The devil speaks in him.

Prospero   No.

For you, most wicked sir, whom to call brother   130
Would even infect my mouth, I do forgive
Thy rankest fault, – all of them; and require
My dukedom of thee, which perforce, I know,
Thou must restore.

Alonso   If thou be'st Prospero,

Give us particulars of thy preservation,
How thou hast met us here, who three hours since
Were wreck'd upon this shore, where I have lost –
How sharp the point of this remembrance is! –
My dear son Ferdinand.

Prospero   I am woe for't sir.

Alonso   Irreparable is the loss, and patience   140
Says it is past her cure.

Prospero   I rather think

You have not sought her help, of whose soft grace
For the like loss I have her sovereign aid,
And rest myself content.

Alonso   You the like loss?

Prospero   As great to me, as late, and, supportable
To make the dear loss, have I means much weaker
Than you may call to comfort you, for I
Have lost my daughter.

---

139. **woe:** sorry

Alonso	A daughter?

O heavens, that they were living both in Naples,
The King and Queen there! That they were, I wish   150
Myself were mudded in that oozy bed
Where my son lies. When did you lose your
   daughter?

Prospero   In this last tempest. I perceive these lords   [153-57]
At this encounter do so much admire,
That they devour their reason, and scarce think
Their eyes do offices of truth, their words
Are natural breath. But, howsoe'er you have
Been justled from your senses, know for certain
That I am Prospero, and that very duke
Which was thrust forth of Milan, who most strangely   160
Upon this shore, where you were wreck'd, was landed,
To be the lord on 't. No more yet of this,
For 'tis a chronicle of day by day,
Not a relation for a breakfast, nor
Befitting this first meeting. Welcome, sir,
This cell's my court. Here have I few attendants,
And subjects none abroad. Pray you look in.
My dukedom since you have given me again,
I will requite you with as good a thing,
At least bring forth a wonder, to content ye   170
As much as me my dukedom.

Here Prospero discovers Ferdinand and Miranda,
playing at chess   [Scene 22]

Miranda   Sweet lord, you play me false.
Ferdinand   No, my dear'st love,
I would not for the world.
Miranda   Yes, for a score of kingdoms you should wrangle,
And I would call it fair play.
Alonso   If this prove
A vision of the island, one dear son
Shall I twice lose
Sebastian   A most high miracle!
Ferdinand   Though the seas threaten, they are merciful.

	I have curs'd them without cause. *Kneels*	
Alonso	Now all the blessings	
	Of a glad father compass thee about!	180
	Arise, and say how thou cam'st here.	
Miranda	O, wonder!	

I have curs'd them without cause.   *Kneels*

Alonso   Now all the blessings
Of a glad father compass thee about!   180
Arise, and say how thou cam'st here.

Miranda   O, wonder!
How many goodly creatures are there here!
How beauteous mankind is! O brave new world,
That has such people in 't!

Prospero   'Tis new to thee.

Alonso What is this maid, with whom thou wast at play?
Your eld'st acquaintance cannot be three hours.
Is she the goddess that hath sever'd us,
And brought us thus together?

Ferdinand   Sir, she is mortal;
But, by immortal Providence, she's mine.
I chose her when I could not ask my father   190
For his advice, nor thought I had one. She
Is daughter to this famous Duke of Milan,
Of whom so often I have heard renown,
But never saw before; of whom I have
Receiv'd a second life; and second father
This lady makes him to me.

Alonso   I am hers.
But, O, how oddly will it sound, that I
Must ask my child forgiveness!

Prospero   There, sir, stop.
Let us not burthen our remembrance with
A heaviness that's gone.

Gonzalo   I have inly wept,   200
Or should have spoke ere this. Look down, you gods,
And on this couple drop a blessed crown!
For it is you that have chalk'd forth the way
Which brought us hither.

Alonso   I say, Amen, Gonzalo!

Gonzalo Was Milan thrust from Milan, that his issue
Should become kings of Naples? O, rejoice
Beyond a common joy, and set it down
With gold on lasting pillars. In one voyage
Did Claribel her husband find at Tunis,

---

199. **burthen:** burden

And Ferdinand, her brother, found a wife   210
Where he himself was lost; Prospero his dukedom
In a poor isle; and all of us ourselves,
When no man was his own.

Alonso   (*to Ferdinand and Miranda*) Give me your hands.
Let grief and sorrow still embrace his heart
That doth not wish you joy!

Gonzalo   Be it so! Amen!

*Re-enter Ariel, with the Master and Boatswain
amazedly following*

O, look, sir, look, sir! Here is more of us!
I prophesied, if a gallows were on land,
This fellow could not drown. Now, blasphemy,
That swear'st grace o'erboard, not an oath on shore?
Hast thou no mouth by land? What is the news?   220

Boatswain The best news is, that we have safely found
Our King and company; the next, our ship –
Which, but three glasses since, we gave out split –
Is tight, and yare, and bravely rigg'd, as when
We first put out to sea.

Ariel   (*aside to Prospero*) Sir, all this service
Have I done since I went.

Prospero   (*aside to Ariel*) My tricksy spirit!

Alonso These are not natural events, they strengthen
From strange to stranger. Say, how came you hither?

Boatswain If I did think, sir, I were well awake,
I'ld strive to tell you. We were dead of sleep,   230
And, how we know not, all clapp'd under hatches,
Where, but even now, with strange and several noises
Of roaring, shrieking, howling, jingling chains,
And mo diversity of sounds, all horrible,
We were awak'd; straightway, at liberty;
Where we, in all her trim, freshly beheld
Our royal, good, and gallant ship, our Master
Capering to eye her – on a trice, so please you,
Even in a dream, we were divided from them,
And were brought moping hither.

---

224. **yare:** seaworthy	238. **capering:** leap for joy	240. **moping:** in a state
234. **mo:** more	**on a trice:** instantly	of bewilderment

Ariel	*(aside to Prospero)* Was't well done? 240
Prospero	*(aside to Ariel)* Bravely, my diligence. Thou shalt be free.
Alonso	This is as strange a maze as e'er men trod,
	And there is in this business more than nature
	Was ever conduct of. Some oracle
	Must rectify our knowledge.
Prospero	Sir, my liege,
	Do not infest your mind with beating on
	The strangeness of this business. At pick'd leisure,
	Which shall be shortly single, I'll resolve you,
	Which to you shall seem probable, of every 250
	These happen'd accidents. Till when, be cheerful,
	And think of each thing well. *(aside to Ariel)* Come hither, spirit.
	Set Caliban, and his companions free.
	Untie the spell. *(exit Ariel.)* How fares my gracious sir?
	There are yet missing of your company
	Some few odd lads that you remember not.

Re-enter Ariel, driving in Caliban, Stephano, and   [Scene 23]
Trinculo, in their stolen apparel

Stephano	Every man shift for all the rest, and let no man take care of himself, for all is but fortune. – Coragio, bully-monster, coragio!
Trinculo	If these be true spies which I wear in my head, here's 260 a goodly sight!
Caliban	O Setebos, these be brave spirits indeed!
	How fine my master is! I am afraid
	He will chastise me.
Stephano	Ha, ha!
	What things are these my lord Antonio?
	Will money buy 'em?
Antonio	Very like. One of them
	Is a plain fish, and, no doubt, marketable.
Prospero	Mark but the badges of these men, my lords,
	Then say if they be true. This mis-shapen knave,

---

249. **single:** private

268. **badges:** Articles of clothing that indicate to whom the servants belong

	His mother was a witch, and one so strong 270
	That could control the moon, make flows, and ebbs,
	And deal in her command, without her power.
	These three have robb'd me, and this demi-devil,
	For he's a bastard one, had plotted with them
	To take my life. Two of these fellows you
	Must know and own, this thing of darkness I
	Acknowledge mine.
Caliban	I shall be pinch'd to death.
Alonso	Is not this Stephano, my drunken butler?
Sebastian	He is drunk now, where had he wine?
Alonso	And Trinculo is reeling ripe. Where should they 280
	Find this grand liquor that hath gilded 'em?
	How cam'st thou in this pickle?
Trinculo	I have been in such a pickle since I saw you last, that
	I fear me will never out of my bones. I shall not fear [284-85]
	fly-blowing.
Sebastian	Why, how now, Stephano?
Stephano	O, touch me not, – I am not Stephano, but a cramp!
Prospero	You'ld be King o' the isle, sirrah?
Stephano	I should have been a sore one, then.
Alonso	This is a strange thing as e'er I look'd on. 290

Pointing to Caliban

Prospero	He is as disproportion'd in his manners
	As in his shape. Go, sirrah, to my cell.
	Take with you your companions. As you look
	To have my pardon, trim it handsomely.
Caliban	Ay, that I will. And I'll be wise hereafter,
	And seek for grace. What a thrice-double ass
	Was I to take this drunkard for a god,
	And worship this dull fool!
Prospero	Go to, away!
Alonso	Hence, and bestow your luggage where you found it.
Sebastian	Or stole it, rather. *Exeunt Caliban, Stephano, and Trinculo* 300
Prospero	Sir, I invite your Highness, and your train
	To my poor cell, where you shall take your rest
	For this one night, which, part of it, I'll waste

282. **pickle:** predicament

99

With such discourse as, I not doubt, shall make it
Go quick away: The story of my life,
And the particular accidents gone by
Since I came to this isle. And in the morn
I'll bring you to your ship, and so to Naples,
Where I have hope to see the nuptial
Of these our dear-belov'd solemnized,   310
And thence retire me to my Milan, where
Every third thought shall be my grave.

Alonso   I long
To hear the story of your life, which must
Take the ear strangely.

Prospero   I'll deliver all,
And promise you calm seas, auspicious gales,
And sail so expeditious, that shall catch
Your royal fleet far off. (*aside to Ariel*) My Ariel,
    chick,
That is thy charge. Then to the elements
Be free, and fare thou well! Please you, draw near.

Exeunt

314. **take:** captivate   ◀ **Caliban and Prospero**

Epilogue

Spoken by Prospero

Now my charms are all o'erthrown,
And what strength I have's mine own,
Which is most faint. Now, 'tis true,
I must be here confin'd by you,
Or sent to Naples. Let me not,
Since I have my dukedom got,
And pardon'd the deceiver, dwell
In this bare island by your spell,
But release me from my bands
With the help of your good hands.   10
Gentle breath of yours my sails
Must fill, or else my project fails,
Which was to please. Now I want
Spirits to enforce, art to enchant;
And my ending is despair,
Unless I be reliev'd by prayer,
Which pierces so, that it assaults
Mercy itself, and frees all faults.
As you from crimes would pardon'd be,
Let your indulgence set me free.   20

Prospero crowned

Stratford Festival Edition Emendations

In the 1982 Stratford Festival Production of *The Tempest*, the following changes were made in the text for various reasons. Occasionally a new word was interjected in order to complement the action of a scene, or an obscure word was changed to a more accessible equivalent. In both cases, anachronism was avoided by using a word that would have been in use in Shakespeare's time.

Often entire lines were cut. Although their meaning was clear to the actor or to someone reading the words on the page with the aid of a glossary, it was found that certain opaque references interfered with the action of the play.

Although such liberties may startle the purist, they ultimately lead to a greater enjoyment of the play on the part of the general audience.

Act I/*Scene 1*

lines 1-67:

> In the 1982 Stratford Festival production of *The Tempest*, various interjections were added in order to provide a fuller orchestration of voices and to help create the atmosphere of a real shipwreck.

Master   Boatswain!
Boatswain Here Master. What cheer?
Master   Good. Speak to th' mariners. Fall to't, yarely, or we run ourselves aground. Bestir! Bestir!
Boatswain Heigh, my hearts.
Mariner Yare.
Master   Quick!
Boatswain Cheerly, cheerly, my hearts! Yare! Yare!
             Take in the topsail. Tend to the Master's whistle.
             Blow till thou burst thy wind, if room enough!

Enter Alonso, Sebastian, Antonio, Ferdinand, Gonzalo, and others from the stage trap

Boatswain	Keep below.
Mariner	Jesu! Jesu!
Alonso	Good Boatswain, have care. Where's the Master? Play the men.
Boatswain	I pray now, keep below.
Antonio	Where is the Master Boatswain?
Boatswain	Do you not hear him? You mar our labour. Keep your cabins! You do assist the storm.
Gonzalo	Nay, good, be patient.
Boatswain	When the sea is. Hence! What cares these roarers for the name of the King. To cabin.
Sebastian	Dar'st thou.
Antonio	Whoreson!
Boatswain	Silence! Trouble us not.
Gonzalo	Good, yet remember whom thou hast aboard.
Boatswain	None that I more love than myself. You are a counsellor. If you can command these elements to silence, and work the peace of the present, we will not hand a rope more. Use your authority. Give thanks you have lived so long, and make yourself ready in your cabin for the mischance of the hour, if it so hap. Cheerly, good hearts.
Mariner	Let go!
Mariner	My children!
Boatswain	Out of our way, I say!
Gonzalo	I have great comfort from this fellow. Methinks he hath no drowning mark upon him. His complexion is perfect gallows. Stand fast, good Fate, to his hanging. Make the rope of his destiny our cable, for our own doth little advantage. If he be not born to be hanged, our case is miserable.

Exeunt Gonzalo and the other nobles

Boatswain	Down with the topmast!
Mariner	Aye. Aye.
Boatswain	Yare! Lower, Lower! Bring her to try with the main course.
Woman	My child!
Woman	My God!
Woman	Jesu, Jesu!
Boatswain	A plague upon this howling! They are louder than the weather, or our office.

Enter Sebastian, Antonio, and Gonzalo

Boatswain	Yet again?
Sebastian	A pox on your throat!
Boatswain	What do you here?
Antonio	You bawling.
Boatswain	Shall we give o'er and drown?
	Have you a mind to sink?
Sebastian	You blasphemous, incharitable dog.
Boatswain	Work you then.
Antonio	Hang, cur, hang, you whoreson, insolent noisemaker! We are less afraid to be drowned than thou art.
Gonzalo	I'll warrant him for drowning, though the ship were no stronger than a nutshell.
Boatswain	Lay her a-hold.
Mariners	Aye! Aye!
Boatswain	A-hold!
Mariners	Aye! Aye!
Boatswain	Set her two courses!
Mariner	Two courses!
Boatswain	Off to sea again! Lay her off!
Mariner	Lost! All lost!
Mariner	To prayers, to prayers!
Mariner	All lost!
Boatswain	What must our mouths be cold?
Gonzalo	The King and Prince at prayers, let's assist them, for our case is as theirs.
Sebastian	I'm out of patience.
Antonio	We are merely cheated of our lives by drunkards, This wide-chopp'd rascal – would thou mightst lie drowning The washing of ten tides!
Gonzalo	He'll be hanged yet, though every drop of water swear against it.
Mariner	Mercy on us! We split, we split! Farewell, my wife and children! Farewell, brother! We split, we split, we split!
Antonio	Let's all sink wi' th' King.
Sebastian	Let's take our leave of him.
Gonzalo	Now would I give a thousand furlongs of sea for an acre of barren ground. Long heath, brown furze, anything. The wills above be done, but I would fain die a dry death.

Act I/*Scene 2*

line 64:
> *teen* was changed to *pain* for clarity.

line 248:
> The second *thee* was cut.

lines 261 and 265:
> *Argier* was changed to *Algier*.

line 351:
> In the Globe Text and in many others, this speech is transferred from Miranda to Prospero, presumably because the harsh tone is out of context with her character. Or perhaps, as Northrop Frye suggests, 19th-century critics did not think these sentiments were appropriate for a lady. Although Miranda is echoing her father, this speech is also indicative of her "education."

line 477:
> Miranda interjected "Father" after the word "imposter."

line 501:
> Miranda interjected "Father" after "Come, follow."

Act II/*Scene 1*

0:
> See note for line 108.

line 35:
> In the Folio, Sebastian laughs and Antonio remarks, "So, you're paid." In the Globe Text both the laughter and the line are attributed to Sebastian. For the Stratford Festival production, Antonio laughed, since he won the bet by wagering on "the cockerel" and Sebastian responded, "So, you're paid."

lines 62 – 64:
> "If but one . . . his report." Sebastian makes a pun on a secondary meaning of pocket: to accept without resentment or to "swallow." These lines were cut.

lines 82 – 83:
> "His word . . . houses too." The miraculous harp of Amphion, which raised the wall of Thebes. A further reference to Gonzalo's mistaking Carthage for Tunis and his ability to create a city simply by talking. These lines were cut.

lines 85 – 90:
> "I think . . . in good time." Gonzalo will create more islands as he has created a new city. These lines were cut.

line 95:
> *Bate* was changed to *except. Widow Dido:* according to Northrope

Frye, "If you find anywhere in Shakespeare a passage of dialogue which is pure blither . . . that is probably where the essential meaning of the play is to be found. *The Tempest*'s literary context, Virgil's *Aeneid*, is suggested by this reference to Dido, and by Gonzalo's wrong assertion that Tunis, where they have just been, is the same city as Carthage, the city where Aeneis left from, leaving Dido to burn herself up on a funeral pyre." *The Tempest* is a story of passing through one kind of life into another, as Aeneas' descent into the lower world was.

line 108:

The character of Francisco was not included in this production and his lines throughout the play were given to Adrian.

line 112:

bold was changed to *brave*.

lines 121 – 122:

"Where she . . . grief on't". Alonso will never see Claribel again. These lines were cut.

lines 125 – 127:

"and the fair . . . should bow." Claribel only went through with the marriage out of obedience to her father. These lines were cut.

line 135:

chirurgeonly was changed to *surgeonly*.

lines 219 – 220:

"how . . . invest it." A play on "stripping," meaning both to denude and to divest of attributes, and "invest" meaning both to clothe and to endow with power. These lines were cut.

lines 223 – 225:

"The setting . . . to yield." Sebastian sees that it is difficult for Antonio to say what is on his mind. These lines were cut.

lines 229 – 230:

"For he's . . . persuade." These lines were cut.

lines 234 – 237:

"No hope . . . there." Ambition itself could not imagine a glory greater than the Throne of Naples, and doubts that such a glory exists. These lines were cut.

Act II/*Scene 2*

line 32:

doit was changed to *penny*.

line 106:

siege was changed to *turd*.

line 127:

Here was cut.

Act III/*Scene 1*

line 15:

> "Most busy lest when I do it." In the Folio and the Globe texts, this line reads "Most busy, lest when I do it." The general consensus is that there is a corruption of the text here, and there is no satisfactory or generally accepted emendation. The New Temple Edition offers the explanation that *busylest* is a possible Shakespearean spelling of *busiliest*. For this explanation to work, the comma must therefore be dropped.

Act III/*Scene 3*

line 107:

> *them swiftly* was changed to *the King*.

line 108 and 109:

> *them* was changed to *him*.

Act IV/*Scene 1*

lines 60 – 138:

> The origin of the masque has been lost in obscurity, but the general consensus is that it is somehow connected with primitive religious rites and folk ceremonies. The fairy tale quality of *The Tempest* is heightened in The Masque scene through the use of music, song, and dance. In the 1982 Stratford Festival production, Ariel's song was written by director John Hirsch. The lyrics echo Aeneas's voyage to the underworld in the sixth book of the *Aeneid*, and Tamino's ordeal through fire and water in *The Magic Flute*.

Ariel   Into the earth you shall go
          Through roots and rocks.
          Sleeping seeds and waking worms
          Shall protect you on your way.

          Into fire you shall go
          Through sparks and flames,
          Damned sinners, tortured souls
          Shall implore you on your way.

Into water you shall go
Through floods and waves,
Pure heart children, cleansed souls
Shall rejoice and sing your way.

Up in air shall you rise
Through crystal spheres and stars,
Wisdom, truth, and soul's delight
Awaits you at the seventh gate.

Ferdinand This is a most majestic vision, and
Harmonious charmingly. May I be bold
To think these spirits?
Prospero   Spirits, which by mine art
I have from their confines called to enact
My present fancies.
Ferdinand   Let me live here ever.
So rare a wondered father and a wise
Makes this place Paradise.
Prospero Sweet, now, silence.
There's something else to do. Hush and be mute,
Or else our spell is marr'd.
Iris Ceres, most bounteous lady, thy rich leas
Of wheat, rye, barley, vetches, oats and peas;
The Queen o' th' sky,
Whose wat'ry arch and messenger am I,
Bids thee leave these, and with her sovereign grace
Here on this grass plot, in this very place,
To come and sport;
Approach, rich Ceres, her to entertain.
Ceres Hail, many-coloured messenger,
Who, with saffron wings, upon my flowers
Diffusest honey-drops, refreshing showers;
Why hath thy Queen summon'd me hither
To this short-grassed green?
Iris A contract of true love to celebrate,
And some donation freely to bestow
On the blessed lovers.
Ceres Great Juno comes. I know her by her gait.
Juno Come with me
To bless this twain, that they may prosperous be,
And honoured their issue.

You sunburned sicklemen, of August weary,
Come hither from the furrow, and be merry.
Be merry, be merry, be merry, be merry,
Make holiday, make holiday, make holiday.

Chorus Honour, riches, marriage blessing,
Long continuance, and increasing,
Juno sings her blessings on you.

Earth's increase, foison plenty,
Barns and garners never empty,
Vines and clustering bunches growing,
Plants with goodly burden bowing;
Spring come to you at the farthest
In the very end of harvest.
Scarcity and want shall shun you,
Iris' blessing so is on you.

Earth's increase, foison plenty,
Barns and garners never empty,
Vines with clustering bunches growing,
Plants with goodly burden bowing;
Spring come to you at the farthest
In the very end of harvest.
Scarcity and want shall shun you,
Ceres' blessing so is on you.

line 226:
   O King Stephano was cut.
lines 236 – 238:
   "Now is . . . bald jerkin." The joke is obscure, but may refer to the
   tale that sailors crossing the equator, or line, proverbially lost their
   hair from scurvy. These lines were cut.
lines 239 – 240:
   "an't like your grace" was cut.
lines 243 – 244:
   "Steal by line . . . garment for't." Stephano is amused by Trinculo's
   "pass of pate" or, "show of wit," and rewards him with a garment.
   These lines were cut.

Act V/*Scene 1*

line 84:

> *hat* changed to *crown*.

lines 153 – 157:

> "I perceive . . . natural breath." The court party is standing in disbelief, with their mouths agape, thus "devour their reason." These lines were cut.

line 284 – 285:

> "I shall not fear fly-blowing." He is so "preserved in alcohol" that flies will not come near him. These lines were cut.

Miranda and Prospero

The stage of the
Stratford Festival Theatre

Biographical Notes

John Hirsch

Artistic Director John Hirsch directed *As You Like It* and *Tartuffe* for the 1983 Stratford Festival season. His other Stratford credits include *The Tempest* and *Mary Stuart*, 1982; *The Three Sisters*, 1976; *Hamlet* and *Satyricon*, 1969; *A Midsummer Night's Dream* and *The Three Musketeers*, 1968; *Richard III* and *Colours in the Dark*, 1967; *Henry VI*, 1966; and *The Cherry Orchard*, 1965.

Mr. Hirsch immigrated to Canada from Hungary in 1947. After graduating from the University of Manitoba he co-founded the Manitoba Theatre Centre and Winnipeg's Rainbow Stage. Former Consulting Artistic Director of the Seattle Repertory Theatre, he has staged productions at major theatres in North America, including the Guthrie Theater in Minneapolis.

He has won the Outer Circle Critics' Award for *St. Joan* at the Lincoln Center Repertory Theater, New York; an Obie Award for *AC-DC* at Brooklyn's Chelsea Theatre; and the Los Angeles Drama Critics' Award for *The Dybbuk* at the Mark Taper Forum, a work he also translated and adapted, and which brought him the Canadian Authors' Association Literary Award. His latest production at the Mark Taper was *Number Our Days*. He has also directed Verdi's *The Masked Ball* at the New York City Opera and Joseph Heller's *We Bombed in New Haven* on Broadway.

As former head of CBC Television Drama, Mr. Hirsch developed many outstanding drama projects, among them *A Gift to Last*, for which he received the Prix Anik Award; *For the Record*; *King of Kensington*; and *Sarah*, starring Zoe Caldwell, which was nominated for an International Emmy Award.

Mr. Hirsch is a member of the Order of Canada.

Desmond Heeley

Desmond Heeley created designs for *As You Like It* and *The Country Wife*, which marked his 25th production for the Stratford Festival since 1957. He also designed the stage itself for the Third Stage. During his illustrious career Mr. Heeley has worked for most major theatre, opera, and ballet companies throughout Europe, Canada, and the United States, and won two Tony Awards for the Broadway production of *Rosencrantz and Guildenstern* in 1967. His most memorable Festival productions include *Arms and the Man*, 1982; *Coriolanus*, 1981; *Titus Andronicus*, 1978-80; *She Stoops to Conquer*, 1972-73; *The Duchess of Malfi*, 1971; *Cyrano*, 1962: and *Hamlet*, 1957.

His most current work includes Lance Mulcahy's *Sweet Will* in Toronto, a "marvellous" musical cabaret of Shakespeare's songs; and a new production of *La Sylphide* for Eric Bruhn, Baryshnikov, and the American Ballet Theatre, which opened in New York in June, 1983.

Michal Schonberg

Michal Schonberg is the Literary Manager of the Stratford Festival. His responsibilities include all the literary matters of the theatre, contacts with playwrights, scholars, and lecturers, as well as consultation on repertory. He is also co-editor of The Stratford Festival Edition of *The Tempest, Macbeth, As You Like It,* and *The Taming of the Shrew.* Associate Professor of Drama and Co-ordinator of Drama Studies at Scarborough College, University of Toronto, Mr. Schonberg has translated several works from Czech into English. He has also translated two of Tom Stoppard's plays, *Every Good Boy Deserves Favour* and *Professional Foul,* into Czech. He co-edited John Hirsch's adaptation of *The Dybbuk* for publication and has had several works and adaptations published in *World Literature Today* and *Modern Drama.* Mr. Schonberg prepared the 1982 Stratford version of *Mary Stuart* with translator Joe McClinton.

Elliott Hayes

Elliott Hayes is the Assistant Literary Manager of The Stratford Festival. For the 1982 Festival Season he was assistant director of *Arms and the Man*, and editor and writer of additional material for *A Variable Passion*. In 1973 he was assistant director of *The Marriage Brokers* at Stratford. A Stratford native, Mr. Hayes trained for three years at the Bristol Old Vic Theatre School in England. He was co-director of *The Caucasian Chalk Circle* and *A Midsummer Night's Dream* for the Verde Valley School in Arizona. Mr. Hayes has staged readings of original poetry, and his play *Summer and Fall* was workshopped at Stratford in 1981. In the 1983 Stratford season his play *Blake* was presented on The Third Stage, with Douglas Campbell in the *tour-de-force* role. Mr. Hayes is co-editor of the Stratford Festival Edition of *The Tempest, Macbeth, As You Like It*, and *The Taming of the Shrew*.

Ferdinand